PETER ALLISS
AND
MIKE WADE
THE LAZY GOLFER'S COMPANION

This edition published in 1995 by
CollinsWillow
an imprint of HarperCollins *Publishers*
London

© Peter Alliss and Mike Wade 1995

A CIP catalogue record for this book is
available from the British Library.

ISBN 0 00 218708 6

Illustrations by Bruce Allard

Produced by Roeder Publications Pte. Ltd.,
179 River Valley Road, Singapore 0617

Printed by Star Standard Pte Ltd, Singapore

PETER ALLISS
THE LAZY GOLFER'S COMPANION

PETER ALLISS AND MIKE WADE

CollinsWillow

An Imprint of HarperCollins*Publishers*

PETER ALLIS WITH ARNOLD PALMER.

FOREWORD

I've known Peter Alliss for almost 35 years. We first met in 1960 Open Championship at St Andrews and then played against each other in the 1961 Ryder Cup at Royal Lytham. It was a terrific battle, which fittingly ended in a draw, and from then on our friendship grew.

Over the years, we have often discussed the great game of golf in all its details. We both agree that the average club golfer makes it much more difficult than it is. For one thing, he does not work at it, although in many cases the available facilities are not very generous and that discourages practice. But very few golfers have the right mental approach to the game, which brings success at club level in both medal and matchplay.

This is why this book is so important for the average golfer. Its sound instruction on clubs, swing problems (with 'quick fixes') and shotmaking techniques (from driving to putting) is very valuable. Its thoughtful advice on the mental side (especially on course management and matchplay tactics) is invaluable. All in all, it will help any golfer to improve his game quite dramatically.

Arnold Palmer

CONTENTS

A TYPICAL WEEKEND FOURBALL

It is 09.48 on a sunny Saturday; the scene of a typical club fourball, almost anywhere in the world. On the first tee, Doug and Brian have been loitering around for four or five minutes, swishing the odd club and talking *sotto voce* about share prices. With one eye on the clock, as their starting time is 09.50 (where on earth are Matt and Bob?) they are also wondering if they will finish the round in time for a leisurely drink. The ritual session at the nineteenth is indispensable for all.

The 'early birds', an assorted bunch of club members who tee off often at first light (possibly because wives demand they are back in "reasonable" time for shopping, visits or even gardening) are well over the horizon. Moodily they watch the four in front criss-crossing the fairway in the mid-foreground at an agonisingly slow amble.

They turn at the squeak of a trolley behind. Matt puffs up followed closely by Bob, who is struggling into a sleeveless sweater. "Had to stop at the garage," he says. "*Just* in time, as usual."

They toss their balls for partners, the two lying closest together playing together and Bob draws Doug, as he feels he does far too often. They are a well (or ill-) matched pair. Bob habitually slices, while Doug mostly has a horrendous hook (not surprising as you couldn't hammer a nail in with his right hand under grip).

TOO MANY THOUGHTS CAN FREEZE THE SWING.

Bob, having the honour, tees up first and squints down the fairway. The four figures in front have now advanced some three hundred yards. "Safe enough to drive off, I suppose?" He looks balefully at the shallow bunker to the right, one hundred and seventy yards out. Nine times out of ten that's where his drives at this hole end up . . . but he ignores it.

Squaring his stance, sucking in his stomach as much as possible, he aligns down the dead centre of the fairway, waggling his driver thoughtfully. Then he freezes for several seconds, swing 'thoughts' jostling in his mind.

Hover the clubhead behind the ball (like Greg). *Back low and slow* (like Nick). *Cock the wrists easily* (like Seve). *Coil fully around* (like John Daly). *Drive with the knees* (like Jack). *Finish high* (like Matt – who has been telling him to for the last six weeks).

His resulting swing is not a thing of beauty. It is cumbersome, at best. The ball, powdered by the dust of a small divot, squirts off centre-rightish and rolls across the right hand edge of the bunker. Behind him Doug grunts "Shot". At least the ball missed the bunker.

The others tee off with similarly predictable results. Doug a long way and deep into the left rough; Brian in the right bunker and Matt (who keeps telling them for quite a while after that he's lifting his head) a topped 'worker' centre-right. Happily off without any disasters (as members of the next fourball are approaching the tee) they move after their drives, talking amiably. Another typical weekend fourball ready to enjoy a pleasant round.

ALWAYS TAKE A WEDGE FROM DEEP ROUGH.

But do they have fun? Well of course they enjoy the next four hours or so, after a fashion. Golf is a fulfilling, pleasurable game and around about the sixteenth, with a couple of balls on the match and one pair playing as many indifferent shots as the other, the competition is satisfying. It would be a lot more fun though if all competed better, if all played as well as they thought they were capable of playing.

They could too . . . with just a little thought and a little careful preparation, which is how this book will help you if you are a high-handicapper, whether you're a municipal or a club golfer. It is not written for the absolute beginner, nor for the player who believes that he can emulate Greg, Payne, Nick or Seve. It is written for the golfer who has been playing for a few (or many) years. It won't change your swing dramatically, but it will help you to lessen its most negative effects. It won't necessarily get you pin high out of a bunker, but it will help you get out. Above all, it will help you to play better, and score better which means you should get a lot more fun out of your golf.

Much of our advice may appear to be just common sense. But common sense and clear thought appear to desert the majority of normally intelligent club golfers the minute they head for the course.

Now there are an estimated seven million golfers in Europe, including small active contingents on the fringes in countries like Hungary and Estonia, and some 24 million in the USA. It is hard to compile the many millions who play along the Pacific Rim, largely because a majority of Japanese golfers play their game mainly on driving ranges, but all club players have certain common factors, world-wide. Their average handicap is 20 – and 80 per cent slice.

Many are desk-bound and overweight. They practice little and rarely improve, yet they are very keen supporters of the game. They buy lots of equipment, attend championships, scrutinise golf books, videos and magazines (from which they glean 'tips' which they apply haphazardly for a couple of rounds). They also get invited occasionally, through a friendly sponsoring company, to play in Pro-Ams.

There are Pro-Ams on the day before most tournaments, which give the Tour pro a chance to practice on the course and earn some valuable prize money as well. So Tour pros sum up the abilities of their (usually three) Pro-Am partners fairly quickly. None of them can damage the team's (pro's) score, but if one or two can improve it on a hole where their handicaps count, it's worthwhile. As a result, on the first tee the pros watch 'their' amateurs like hawks. By the fifth or sixth hole they offer a little advice here and there which starts to bring about the odd par where bogey had been the norm.

The pro would have had a few pithy things to say to the members of our fourball after the first 380 yards par four hole. Something diplomatic to Bob (who with 200 yards to go had taken a 3-iron, never having hit one more than 180 yards, and had buried his ball in knee-high rough short on the right) like: "Don't swing your *body* at the ball. Try and hit it with your hands and arms instead." Or to Brian (who had taken two to get out of the bunker) like: "Don't

CASUAL GOLFERS ARE KEEN SUPPORTERS AT THE GAME.

try and *lift* the ball off the sand. Take plenty of it." Or to Doug (who had tried a 4-iron out of deep to advance it 25 yards) like: "Next time use your *wedge* and aim for the nearest bit of fairway."

With Matt he would be reserving judgment because after another skinny one, Matt had pitched to the fringe and fired a putt that rocketed in off the pin. His fluky par won the hole over two bogeys and a double. They had all left the green happily. Things would certainly improve once they got into their game.

How different it could all have been. Bob's dream when he stood on the first tee (sorry to be picking on him but he's a good example of a typical club player), was to crack a drive quail-high 250 yards down the middle. The reality we know, but with a little common sense he could have played the hole much better, while *making the best* of what he had in terms of swing and ability.

First, arriving "just in time" without a chance to loosen up virtually guarantees a cranky shot. That is not to say you should spend half an hour on the practice ground before every round: in the time-stressed 1990s few have time to spare and club golfers mostly hate practising. And indeed, how many golf clubs in the UK have decent practice facilities of any sort? But virtually everyone has played tennis at some time. Would you consider going straight onto a court and with your first movement hit a serve in the first 'scoring' game, even if it's a friendly match? Of course not. You'd have a short knock-up first – and that is what club golfers should do, even if it's a few putts on the putting green and a couple of chips.

Second, Bob did not use the grey matter between his ears which constitutes a large part of the simple game of golf. He had been in a bunker at the first nine times out of ten, yet he still aimed *straight* down the fairway. Knowing he always sliced, he should have teed up on the right hand side of the tee and aimed at the left hand rough where Doug ended up. With his usual swing, he would probably have ended up in the middle of the fairway and very likely have hit the ball twenty yards or so further.

Third, no one can swing fluidly, if they have umpteen swing thoughts jostling in their minds. You can never get a natural-looking, effective, repeating swing that way. At the most, you can hold *one* swing thought for the day ("Swing *slower*" is often a good one).

Fourth, Bob's second shot to the green was a combination of nonsense and vanity. Once you've got off the tee, it's the *second* shot that make the difference in scoring for the player. Underclubbing is the major fault (as it often is on long par three holes).

Finally (although there are many other lessons to be learned from this role model performance) Bob took his driver off the first tee. Now it's all very well hitting your *drive* at the start if you've hit quite a few on the practice ground before the game. But in Bob's case, driving off with the most difficult club in his bag did not make sense. Added to which his driver had a swing weight and lie designed for a six foot four, athletic 20-year-old, which Bob certainly is not!

And that brings us to one of the most important factors for the club golfer, the 'tools of the trade' – your golf clubs.

THE A TO Z OF EQUIPMENT

With most sports and many pastimes, the equipment you use can be of prime importance to the way you perform and enjoy yourself. You would not, for example, go jogging in your highly polished brogues; nor would someone of 50 enjoy playing tennis with the heavy wooden (and probably by now decidedly warped) racket he wielded when he was 20. By contrast, he would find playing with a modern large-headed, graphite or aluminium framed racket very much easier. Not to mention much less tiring because of its lighter weight. Shots are crisper, more accurate and accomplished with less effort.

The same can be very true of golf clubs. Yet considering the amount the average golfer 'invests' in the game (in terms of subs or green fees, clothes, shoes, bags, trolleys – and time) it is very surprising how little he or she knows about the clubs they play with. The *right* clubs for a player, suiting his height, weight, age and shape of swing will boost confidence and shot making – although they alone will not cut his handicap. The *wrong* clubs, however, will certainly affect his game adversely and hinder, or even stop, any improvement.

But very few golfers know the swing weight and shaft flex of the clubs which suit them best, or the lie essential to their swing. Clubs, it would seem, are often acquired spontaneously or by chance. What

NEVER PLAY WITH THE WRONG CLUBS FOR YOUR SWING SHAPE.

often happens, as with our fourball, is that Matt will ask Brian on the eighth fairway if he can "try out" his 4-iron. Now Brian had bought his latest 'bargain' set of clubs from the sports department of the local department store just five weeks ago. He'd been enticed by adverts that focused on investment cast, perimeter weighted heads, high-torque graphite shafts with good vibration dampening properties – and a sizeable discount on the set. Since he had bought them, he had been telling anyone who would listen that his shots, particularly the irons, had become much straighter and longer, something he certainly felt even if his scoring had not noticeably improved.

His enthusiasm was most probably due to a) the need to justify the cost of a new set and b) the *initial* confidence that any new club brings. Buying a bargain set of clubs from a sports department is not to be recommended, unless a golfer knows his personal specifications exactly (especially swing weight, flex and lie) and can match them to the clubs. The store's staff may know about equipment in general but it is most unlikely that they would be able to fit out a golfer correctly.

So what happens on the eighth? Matt takes the proffered high-tech club and swings it a few times reflectively. Disregarding the fact that he's a solidly built six foot three, while Brian is a slim five foot five, so the club might not suit him anyway, he addresses the ball and hits it a hundred and fifty odd yards, high and slightly right. "Hmm," he says, handing the club back, "I like the *feel*". Mentally he makes a note that he might just drop into the sports department next week to see if it had any others of the same make in stock.

Brian, who has watched the flight of the ball goggle-eyed, mutters "shot" admiringly. He has never managed to hit a ball so high (it is strange how whenever someone 'borrows' one's clubs they produce results with them very different from one's own). He basks a little in the compliment. Matt likes the 'feel' of his new clubs.

Distance or Control – That Is the Question

The feel of a club clearly seems to be all important. But just what is feel? Well, there is no scientific equation or formula that defines it. All one can say is that the way a golfer feels a club when he swings it depends on its swing weight and the flexibility of its shaft.

Now swing weight is a concept that balances the weight of the grip end (and shaft) of the club to its headweight. It is expressed as an alphabetical and numerical number, such as C8 (a standard for lissome lady players) or D0 (for active men over 50) or D5 (which is about the top limit for powerfully-built under-35s). It is at least an attempt to produce a uniform 'feel' in a set of clubs, despite the difference in their length, which is a major factor in a matched set, the other being the flex of their shafts.

Steel shafts were initially graded by flex, which was defined only by weight. 'L' and 'A' flex shafts were the most flexible, or whippy and the lightest; then came 'R' for regular, 'S' for stiff and the

'X' flexed or stiffest shafts that were the heaviest. Light-weight alloy shafts, which appeared with the high-tech developments in the 1970s, brought other dimensions. Shafts could be stiff, yet light-weight and they had a range of 'flexpoints' (a low flexpoint apparently whips the head of the club through impact giving a higher ball flight). Graphite shafts, the lightest of all with vibration dampening properties, have added new variables. Torque for one. This is the twisting of the shaft as club meets ball. Too much, or too little, torque can make straightening that slice much more difficult. One wonders what Bobby Jones would have made of it all.

Today, shaft selection is a highly confusing, esoteric area. There are more than 100 companies worldwide manufacturing over 10,000 types of shaft. Most produce data where the speed of a golfer's swing helps to choose the 'ideal' shaft for him or her. With a speed of between 65–70 mph, there are some 31 different makes to ponder over. The whole process is far too complicated for the average golfer, who hasn't the time or inclination to get immersed in such technicalities. Fortunately, there are some guidelines to simplify matters.

You should have clubs that you can swing *easily* and fast, which still allow you to control the clubhead within your ideal swing tempo. Now the lighter the clubhead, the faster its speed and the stiffer the shaft, the greater the control. This is why top Tour pros have light-headed drivers with stiffish shafts. They like to feel the club is a solid unit and if a club golfer swings one of their clubs (try one at your next Pro-Am) it's like swishing a cut-down billiard cue. The 'click' as it strikes the ball has much the same sensation as hitting a billiard ball as well. These clubs are designed for powerful professional athletes who can generate high clubhead speed without any help from the flex of the club. They are *not* for the club player.

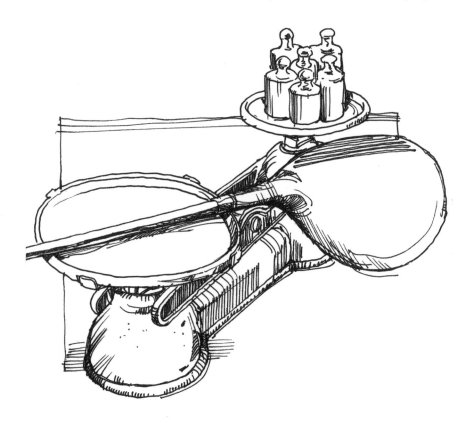

MOST CASUAL GOLFER'S CLUB ARE FAR TOO HEAVY.

Nor is the other extreme of a whippy shaft and a heavy clubhead. With this option, the club will flex more during the swing and you will get more "feel" (which was probably why Matt liked Brian's new four iron). But your timing has to be spot-on. Powerfully built golfers may hit the ball miles with them, but with hardly any control. Heavy clubs are also not suitable for the club golfer and many Tour and teaching pros believe that golfers generally use clubs that are far too heavy (probably because clubhead weight gives a sensation of power).

Shaft flex, however, is important. The more senior, slightly-built golfer (like Brian) who plays an average of once a week, has a limited ability to generate clubhead speed and often has a slow swing tempo with little hand action. A whippy 'A' flex shaft, coupled with a light swing weight of C9, could give a good balance between clubhead speed and control.

Middle-aged sedentary golfers who play regularly (like Doug) often lack real clubhead speed despite having a more powerful physique. In such a case the best balance for performance is generally an 'R' flex shaft with a D0 – D1 swing weight. Finally, for the active players under 50 (particularly for those who have played hockey or cricket in their youth, like Matt) and who tend to hit hard through the ball, an 'S' or stiff flex could be O.K. An 'R' flex might be better, but the swing weight should be kept to between D1 and D3.

The Right Mix of Materials

Once you have decided on the right specs for your clubs, you should be able to get a perfectly matched set easily. You should though be aware that few Tour pros use clubs that are matched, despite the manufacturer's logos worn on bag or visor. Their bags might contain a very stiff, light-headed driver, or a 2-wood which several use for safety, (Bobby Locke setting the precedent,) plus a fairway wood of a different make. There would be a variety of makers' names on the one, three, four and five irons and an equal variation on the soles of the pitching clubs. Locke has found through many hours of practice (which the club golfer abhors) what suits him best.

But are they matched? Well, there is the apocryphal story of Bobby Jones who won 13 majors with a selection of hand-crafted clubs gleaned from all over Britain and the US. Such was his feel for weight and flex that when they were tested, it was said they were perfectly matched – except for one club. "Ah yes," said Jones, "I was never really happy with that niblick" (the equivalent of an 8-iron).

Golf club technology has evolved considerably since the days of Bobby Jones and golfers should be aware of the clubhead options in the 1990s. The shape of clubheads in the 1960's and 1970s (still used by many today) were flat at the back. Forged from mild steel alloys, they were hand beaten out of a mould and gave a "soft feel" on striking the ball. Today's heads are most likely to be cavity backed and investment cast from slightly harder metals. (Sorry if this all sounds too technical, but it has to be explained).

Now investment casting is a process where molten metal is poured into ceramic shells, which are broken when everything cools, resulting in more accurate heads. Cavity backed models are perimeter weighted (the weight is all in the rim) which is said to diminish the effects of off-centre impacts. Their lower centre of gravity gives a higher ball flight and most have a four-way radius (they are bevelled from front to back and heel to toe) which means they should slide easier through the rough.

The lofts of today's clubs (the angle of the club face to the vertical) are also quite a lot stronger than earlier models from the 1970s. Typically, a modern wood will be one degree stronger (a modern three has 16 degrees of loft, compared to 17 degrees for a traditional model). Equally a 1990s 3-iron will have 21 degrees of loft, compared to 24, while all the other modern irons from the four to the pitching wedge are four degrees stronger. This really means that a 1990s 5-iron, with 28 degrees of loft, is equivalent to a 1970s 4-iron. No wonder that modern perimeter weighted clubs with lower centres of gravity and stronger loft shit the ball straighter, higher and further – or at least are supposed to.

But take note – not all club manufacturers have the same loft standards so you must check before you buy. Your club pro should also check your lofts once a year or so, which is something Tour pros do constantly. You can see this whenever you visit a tournament.

Parked, usually beside the practice ground, are two or three exotic converted 'mobile homes', provided by golf club construction companies, which follow the PGA Euro Tour. They are really mobile workshops and they have the club makers logos emblazoned on their sides, plus those of shaft makers and sponsors. There is a constant stream of Tour pros tracking in and out clutching various clubs, often when they've finished their round for the day.

Inside (if you could talk your way in) you would find a well stocked fridge (no alcohol), comfy seats and a TV with video. The rest of the space is a real golfer's workshop, crammed with stacks of shafts, irons, drivers and putters. There is also a machine (often a digital one) that can measure loft to the tenth of a degree and it takes only a few minutes to check any club. Tour pros need to know if their clubs are performing as they should – and the club golfer should seek similar reassurance at least once a year.

After all, with regular play, you could develop a weak 4-iron, a perfect (modern lofted) five and a strong 6-iron which would mean you were carrying three 5-irons.

Green Lies

At least one, if not all, of the mobile workshops have machines 'on board' that will measure a club's lie – a key factor in eventual performance; a point often totally neglected by the club golfer. The lie is the angle between the shaft and the head of the club when it's soled flat on the ground and it can have a critical effect on the direction of the shot, especially with the irons if the toe or the heel of the club make contact with the ground before the ball.

To explain: a tall golfer (like Matt) who stands close to the ball and has a fairly upright swing needs an upright lie (which makes the shaft seem more vertical). If he were to use a club with too flat a lie for his swing, its toe would catch the ground first and its heel would move past it, opening the club face and shooting the ball off right. (This, indeed, is what happened when he tried out Brian's 4-iron which had a one degree flat lie.)

On the other hand, if you have a flattish swing and use a club with an upright lie, its heel would dig into the ground first and the club face would pivot around it, closing through the ball which would be pull-hooked left. This is not to imply that all tall players have upright swings, while shorter ones have flatter ones. It all depends on the length of arms to overall height and the distance a golfer stands away from the ball. But lie is very important and every golfer should know if he or she swings, say, one degree flat or upright, and make sure that the club matches the swing.

One way to find out how steep a lie you need is to hit a number of shots with different clubs from a lie board. Hitting the board marks the bottom of the club at a certain point which, if not along the centre of the sole, shows what's wrong. If the mark is consistently towards the toe of the club, the lie needs to be flatter, while if towards the heel, you need a more upright angle.

So where can you, a club golfer, find a lie board – and how can you determine the optimum flex and swing weight for your very individual swing? Well, your Club pro should be able to help, but he too is faced with a large variety of choices and not too much advice from club makers (who seem to believe that 95 per cent of all golfers are suited by a standard set of their clubs).

WITH TOO FLAT A LIE, THE TOE DIGS IN.

Incidentally, out of eight club manufacturers contacted in mid1994 with a polite request by a golfer for background details or literature on how he could be measured to fit their clubs, only *one* had the courtesy to reply. This is not good PR considering the cost of a new set. Club makers could and should do a lot more to help golfers get the clubs that are best suited to them, but of course they have to rely on the golf professional; very much depends on his ability and interest in making sure that his clients get the right clubs.

The Saville Row Option

Another option for the golfer is the 'Saville Row' or custom-made clubs approach. A visit to a high-tech fitting centre of a custom club supplier (e.g. Petron) is an interesting (and learning) experience for one and all and the resulting clubs, tailored to an individual's swing, are surprisingly not that expensive.

You first make an appointment and turn up at the allotted time with your own set of clubs. These are used as a 'benchmark' against which the new clubs' performance can be measured. You are greeted in a reception area where detailed pre- and post-fitting out analysis takes place and while you are discussing your game with the resident pro, your old clubs are all tested for swing weight, flex, loft and lie on special machines. The results are invariably surprising.

Your driver, which you have never hit with any confidence, turns out to have a swingweight of D0 and is one degree open (no wonder you sliced) while your 5-wood is D2. What you thought was a matched set of irons is utterly inconsistent in weight, totally unmatched. The 4-iron has a swingweight of C3, the 6-iron is A6, the seven is B1 and the sand wedge is D4. There are 29 swingweight differences between them; no wonder your handicap has stayed so high!

The pro then measures you for three important dimensions. First is the distance from your fingertips of both hands to the ground when standing balanced and erect (there's normally a difference of half an inch between them). This is to gauge the right length of club for you and it's worth knowing that 'modern' irons are half an inch longer than those of the 1970s, which should lead to a wider swing arc and more distance, in theory.

Your ideal grip thickness is next assessed, which is not necessarily thicker for larger hands, by measuring how comfortably the club sits when you hold it. Grip size can affect performance and slicers could benefit from thinner grips than they normally use. This tends to make them hold the club more in the fingers, which leads to faster hand action. Conversely, the few golfers who are happy hookers should try grips thicker than their norm. They would find the club sits more in the palm, which slows down the speed the club face closes. You should try this when you next get your grips replaced by your club pro – which you should do at least every two years. Shiny, slippery grips don't help your game and as most golfers are too lazy to wash their grips regularly (let alone sandpaper or scrape them) they have a limited effective life.

We're talking about spending money. It's common sense once you have spent money to look after your equipment and unfortunately golfers are very bad at that. They'll buy a new £150 suit of waterproof clothes, and get them wet. When the sun comes out after about 12 holes, they take their waterproofs off and then, while the material's still wet, stuff it in the golf bag, forget all about it and leave it in the back of the car. Then, of course, when they play the next week, the gear's either got mildew on or it's damaged in some way and they will then complain that they bought a faulty garment which need not necessarily be the case.

Finally, at the centre, you are measured up on a length and lie gauge to find the right angle for your clubs when you are in a comfortable address position. You then move to the driving range, where computers, linked to high-speed cameras, record the results of hitting a number of balls with a selection of carefully-chosen clubs. Typically, a 5-iron is used as a standard club and after a few warm-up shots (hitting balls off a mat into a net five yards away) the computer-camera machine is calibrated.

You then hit four balls, taking your time, with your old 5-iron. Each shot is displayed on a screen showing, by computer enhanced graphics, how far (and with what spin) the ball would have travelled down a fairway. The computer also measures the club speed at impact, ball carry, angle of the club face, swing path, impact point on the club – and tempo of each swing from start to impact.

Warming to the task, you then repeat the four ball series of swings with five different 5-irons, selected by the centre's pro, and varying in flex and swingweight from D0 to C9, C6, C3 to flyweight. Then, perhaps a little impatient to see how you've performed, you return to reception for analysis and detailed explanation.

From the computer print-out of all your shots, the pro shows you that your old 5-iron has generated an average clubhead speed of 76 mph, giving a carry of 170 yards (which makes you feel like Ian Woosnam), a clubhead closed at impact by one degree (which, with your in to out swing, explains the hook) and an impact point in the centre of the club (well at least you're doing something right). The C3 5-iron, with a graphite shaft, has a higher average clubhead speed of 79 mph, but its carry was less at 168 yards and the ball was generally struck near the heel. The featherweight club, strangely enough, only generated an average 75 mph speed and you didn't really like its feel anyway.

One 5-iron in the series really does stand out. It's a perimeter weighted club with a C9 swing weight, an 'R' flex steel shaft and a one degree flat lie. Giving a consistent impact in the centre of the club face, this is clearly the club for you.

So do you immediately reach for the cheque book and order a matched set? Well, there is no hard sell pressure to buy, curiously enough. Custom club suppliers generally like to sell their wares through your club pro – and prefer him to attend the fitting out sessions, if possible. What they do give the golfer is, above all, a

CUSTOM-MADE CLUBS WILL SUIT YOUR SWING.

feeling of confidence that his clubs really suit him and that if he does need a 'Mulligan' on the first tee, he will only have himself to blame.

Club Combinations

Armed with his personal club spec though, there are still other considerations for the golfer to ponder over when it comes to selecting the *combination* of clubs that he carries around. Being long off the tee, or having a short game, can make a difference. Let's see how the members of our fourball could each pick the best mix.

Bob, who is a confirmed slicer, should probably never wield a driver in anger. There's nothing to be ashamed about this; it's merely pragmatic. A 2-wood off the tee, with a modern loft of 13 degrees, will reduce his sidespin and slice. It should have a metal or graphite head, with an 'R' flex steel (or mid torque graphite) shaft. He could also consider carrying a three, a five and a seven wood of similar materials, while his irons should have similar shafts with perimeter weighted heads to aid off-centre hits. Finally, on all of them, he should fit (having tried out first) say one sixteenth of an inch thinner grips, which should increase his hand action.

Brian, who lacks length off the tee, constantly has to hit longer second shots to the greens, needs help from his clubs to gain as much distance as possible. All his shafts should be 'A' flex (or high torque graphite) to give as much 'kick' as possible. He should use a driver and try thinner grips to increase his clubhead speed.

Doug, the rare hooker in our fourball, could consider leaving his driver behind, a 2-wood giving him almost as much distance and probably being straighter off the tee. With 'R' flex shafts in all clubs, he should also carry a 4-wood, which is an excellent club from light rough. He should try slightly oversize grips to help him hold the clubs more in the palm and control his tendency to end up left.

Finally comes Matt, who has a handicap of 16, the lowest of the four. He may need 'S' flex (or low torque graphite) shafts on all his clubs and could sport a driver, three and five woods all with persimmon heads. He could also use forged traditional irons – if he could afford them and if he played more. But then we all need to play a bit more, don't we?

Playing more with the right equipment would benefit, if not the Tour pro. It's sobering to note that, despite modern technology, in mid 1994 the average drive of a player on the US Professional Tour measured some 264 yards, only eight yards more than the average in 1969, 25 years previously. Average US pro scores have fallen by one stroke (to 71) during this period – though many courses have been stretched. However, this has been credited to the fact that players are fitter today, more athletic and have benefitted from more intensive coaching. There is also the considerably greater financial incentives for each tournament. None of this applies to the social golfer, who probably hasn't changed at all in the past 25 years – but high tech clubs would have a positive effect on his game, if only he played with them a more.

Balls for All Needs

But what about that vital complement to any set of clubs, the balls that make the game go round? Well, they can make (or unmake) the player too. There is an enormous choice of golf balls on the market today and you can buy a type that both suits your game and the course you are playing. Too few golfers though know how to make that choice, or even think for a moment about the ammunition they use. Rather like motor cars, there are no bad golf balls now. Some are different and feel better than others, softer, harder, some last longer, some don't cut as easily. But it is quite important and sensible to get a golf ball that suits your game. It can make quite a difference.

The proof is seen in most golfer's bags: a mix of balls, two-piece and wound, with a few balata covers (often cut) and with a variety of compressions and trajectories. How can any golfer hope to play with any consistency with such a mixture? There is no need to.

All the ball manufacturers, in co-operation with golf magazines, regularly publish listings of makes with details of their construction, covers and compressions. There are also charts grouping balls suitable for traditionally forged clubs and perimeter weighted ones; high trajectory balls (if you normally hit them lower than you'd like) and low trajectory types; those suitable for courses with narrow fairways and others with wide open spaces. The weather is also catered for: certain ball types are listed for windy conditions, and others for abnormally dry or very wet ones.

A golfer can gain some useful information from these charts, but there are three points you should bear in mind:

- A balata cover is very soft and if you've got any roughness on the face of your irons or if the grooves in the clubs are a little bit sharp, every time you hit it, even if you strike the ball correctly, you will rough it up as if you've rubbed a file or rasp over the cover and after two or three holes a ball can look very aged indeed. Surlyn is more durable, a little bit stronger.

- You would probably find the use of a 100 compression ball downright off-putting (it's rather like hitting a stone) so use a 90 compression ball and stick with it.

- When you've decided on the optimum ball for your game and course, don't buy any other type. If you find any others in the rough, use them for practice at best.

To sum up and to simplify advice to the club golfer on the tools of the trade, we could say that you owe it to yourself to:

- make certain that your clubs are right for your swing, in terms of swing weight, flex and lie; and

- choose and use only the golf balls that suit your game and your course conditions best.

This will bring you a certain peace of mind when you next tee off. Let's see how you should use this equipment for the best . . .

THE LAZY GOLFER'S SWING
TECHNIQUE

Whenever a real golfer gets a new anything to do with golf (new clubs, a special wedge, the 'ultimate' secret from the latest book, whatever) he can't wait to try it out on the course. But before you trot briskly off to the first, satisfied that at last your clubs and balls really suit you, there are some basics to consider and ponder about. Not least, what *type* of swing have you been using over the last 'x' years?

You do already appreciate that everyone has an individual swing, very individual as you will see if you scrutinise the line of players at a driving range. The world's top Tour pros are also different, if not so divergent, in the overall appearance of their swings. Nick Price, for example, has a decidedly brisk tempo. Fred Couples, on the other hand, swings almost drowsily, lifting the club with his arms, turning his shoulders late and looping the club inside to be on plane at impact. Ian Woosnam seems to stand a long way from the ball, yet he smacks it with very little apparent effort a long way down the fairway, as does Greg Norman, who seems to stand almost on top of the ball, which he assaults with a vigorous, gut-wrenching action.

These four are instantly recognisable by their swings, even at the distance of a well struck drive. Yet they all have in common a sound swing technique which maximises their physical abilities and they are, to a man, top-notch exponents of the 'modern' swing. This is something of prime importance to really understand. For there are two distinct basic types of swing; the classical and the modern.

The Classic and the Not So Classic Swing

Misunderstanding the different principles of the two types (and worse, using bits of one with parts of the other) has wrecked the swings of many golfers – and even a few Tour pros.

The classic swing is more of a hands and arms action (rather than the 'whole body' movement of the modern swing, where the arms follow, rather than lead). Dating from the days of brassies, spoons, cleeks and mashie-niblicks, it was exemplified by the flowing movement of Bobby Jones, who started his swing with the hands leaving the clubhead behind, contrasted to the compact three-quarter action of Sir Henry Cotton.

The classic grip was more in the fingers, promoting a faster hand action, and the classic golfer typically aligned slightly right of the pin and positioned the ball further back in his stance (centre for the 5-iron and even nearer the right foot for the short clubs).

Foot action was also more pronounced, with the left heel lifting high off the ground in the backswing, basically because the thick tweeds the players wore restricted easy movement. The arms were also kept close to the body, the right elbow tucked in at the top, the left on the follow through, and the overall action was quite rotary on a flattish plane. The classic swinger also hit against a 'firm left side' which, with his set-up and swing shape, produced theoretically a right to left shot, hopefully a draw.

The modern swing, in contrast, has much more *emphasis* on body movement. The legs drive, the hips turn, the arms follow and, in theory, the bottom of the arc is extended through impact, keeping closer to the ground for longer and hitting the ball further.

The modern grip is more in the palm of the left hand, more neutral, and exponents talk of "taking their hands out of the game."

CLASSIC OR MODERN: BOTH CAN BE RIGHT FOR YOU.

They align square or more open to the flag and generally position the ball for all clubs (except the driver) some two inches inside the left heel. With lighter, less restrictive clothes, modern swingers roll their left foot on the backswing and stretch their arms a little further away from the body, creating a more lateral and upright swing, with the clubhead travelling more down the line to the target. All this tends to produce, particularly with modern clubs, a higher ball which flies left to right, hopefully as a power fade.

Now what you as a club golfer must further appreciate is that using a hands and arms swing, a classic action, today is not wrong because it is outdated. Equally, it is not imperatively right to use a leg driven modern swing just because most top Tour pros do. The classic swing developed because of the whippy shafted clubs used in earlier times and the need to hit long, low shots under the wind on the firm turfed links. The modern swing is an evolution based on the technology of much stiffer, lighter shafts and the need to hit longer, higher shots, particularly on the stretched, lush courses in the US.

Some top pros appreciated this evolution and quickly adopted it, one being Tony Jacklin. When he started to play on the US Tour in the late 1960's, he had a classic hands and arms swing. But then he studied the action of fellow pros like Jack Nicklaus and Tom Weiskopf and was soon convinced that he was not making adequate use of his legs to suit the courses they played. The change for him, which simply meant bending his knees a bit more and driving with his legs, took quite a time. Teaching pros today advocate practising a swing change sixty times a day for three solid weeks to groove it. For Jacklin, it involved hitting thousands of balls on dozens of practice areas and he believes he ended up with a slower, more rhythmic action which hit the ball further than he'd ever done before.

Doug once tried to change his swing in a similar way, having read of the 'new' Jacklin swing in his favourite golf magazine. He did it in a desperate attempt to cure his hook and hit a few balls on the practice ground one day, taking his remodelled swing onto the course the next. There he found to his horror that he had developed a pernicious push-slice, the ball flying right at forty five degrees to his intended line and then curling even further right, to end usually out-of-bounds, almost level with him. When, in desperation, he tried to revert to his 'old' swing on the eighth, he started to take deep divots, advancing the ball only thirty or forty yards forwards at a time. It took him a month in the end to cure his 'cure'. What he should have realised from the start is that *any* small swing change, never mind a major reconstruction, demands practice, practice and yet more practice before it can begin to work. Doug, as a club golfer, should also have consulted his club pro before he started and have been guided by him throughout the change.

Supertips from Top Pros

With the basic differences between the classic and modern swings however, there is one thing you must be very clear about. The hands and arms alone do not solely create the motive power to propel the ball. The whole body plays a part, while the legs are certainly active, not frozen as some would believe. Equally, with the modern swing, while the lower body drives, the arms must swing down fast and free. Both actions are essential motive forces that add power to the swing, be it classical or modern.

Body power is generated by coiling the upper torso against the resistance caused by a flexed right knee and solid feet – a good foundation is all important. These are released automatically on the downswing. The hand and arm action supplies power to the shot by working as a swinging unit and with both forces, good leg action is essential for rhythm and balance during the swing, but perhaps it is not such an important source of power as some have argued. Try hitting a few balls with a 6-iron with your feet together, knees touching. Seve Ballesteros can hit a ball well over 200 yards on his knees.

So what every golfer should be aiming for, whether he has a classic or modern swing, is a balanced combination of hand and arm action and body action which results in the club face hitting squarely through the ball with maximum speed directly towards the target. It is in trying to get this balance, this *timing*, right that the club golfer can go disastrously wrong.

Too much body action is the major factor that wrecks the timing of many golfers. Often swinging back too far with their hips, with no resistance from knee or feet, they *think* about using their

A SWING CHANGE TAKES A LOT OF PRACTICE.

CUTTING EXCESSIVE BODY ACTION, WITH KNEES TOGETHER.

lower body action too much on the downswing and consequently don't swing their arms freely enough.

One reason for this may stem from TV programmes and videos that analyse the swings of top players in slow motion. The couch golfer watching Couples or Woosnam, say, may note that their lower bodies move towards the ball before their arms seem to start the downswing. Not appreciating the natural fast hand and arm action of the top pros, the golfer copies the body action alone. Worse still, he may copy bits of the swings of different pros, dovetailing some of Couples' technique with parts of Woosnam. In that case he should realise that if Couples tried to copy Woosnam's swing and vice versa, they would probably both have handicaps in double figures.

Copying the top pros without understanding what they are *really* doing has befuddled golfers since the earliest days of the game. There's an inevitability about this search for 'the secret', shown in P G Wodehouse's writings on Sandy MacBean and his book *How to Become a Scratch Man in Your First Season by Studying Photographs*. But today golfers often pick up some very bad habits from trying to copy their favourites – like taking too much time over their shots. They see the Tour professionals preparing to drive, discussing club selection with their caddies, teeing up, putting on their glove and then stepping up to the ball. Then just when you think they're getting ready to strike, they stop and walk behind and check the line again, throw some grass in the air to check the wind and study the tops of the trees before finally taking up their stance. And then, sometimes,

SET A PERSONAL TIME LIMIT FROM THE START OF ADDRESS.

lo and behold, they have a few more practice swings just in case. It's even more protracted on the greens, some professionals stalking the line of their putts clockwise, counter clockwise tapping down pitchmarks, plumb-bob lining up the hole. Several practice putts, another look here, another look there, all adds ten, fifteen, twenty seconds per shot to the round of golf. It's no wonder there are so many five-hour rounds played today.

One of the worst problems today is that people think that if they take a long time, they must be concentrating. That is not the case. This is especially true on the tee, where the club golfer is usually afraid of fooling (something the pro can hardly conceive of). Setting up, the longer he takes, the more likely doubting thoughts can pervade the concentration and wreck the swing. The best advice is to aim for a personal time limit: take twenty seconds say from the moment it's 'your turn' to the moment you pull the trigger. It will clear the mind of random doubts and your probably find you will play a lot better.

Club golfers also copy the way many pros tee the ball low. The pros do this to promote a powerful fade and a low tee is definitely not for the player who slices. Nor is a ball position that is off the left heel for all clubs. This is fine for the Tour pro with his strong leg driven modern swing, but with the average golfer it only leads to excessive body action and problems.

If the golfer is to copy anything from his favourite pro, aside from enjoying his play hopefully, it should be his free arm swing.

This is the unbalanced motive force in the majority of golfers' swings, especially those who slice. Yet most fit people can swing the clubhead fast enough with their hands and arms to play reasonable golf.

This does *not* imply that club golfers should adopt a classic swing technique, hitting against a firm left side. Nor is there any suggestion that if you have been playing for quite a few years and have a middling handicap, you should try to change your swing radically. However, it may be beneficial to consider a sound swing technique that would suit the average golfer. If you adopt some of its elements into the golf swing you already have, you could see some very positive results. It ought to be said that all golf swings are like finger prints, every one is different. You can mentally feel that you're copying somebody's swing: the tempo's the same, your walk, your every mannerism, is a carbon copy of your hero. But in reality it's not like that at all, you're born with your own rhythm of life and that is carried through into the game of golf.

GASP

To start with, every golfer must have a pre-shot routine, where he takes a grip on the chosen club and sets up to the ball. If you have a grip that's right for your swing and a comfortably correct set-up, you are 90 per cent on the way to hitting a good golf shot. But if your grip and set-up are faulty you are virtually guaranteeing a bad one.

Pros can tell at a glance if a golfer has a low, a middle or a high handicap just from his address routine. The low handicapper, having taken an easy practice swing and checked the line of the shot, moves positively to the ball. He aims the club face, aligns his body and settles comfortably for the shot. The high handicapper, in contrast, usually looks tense over the ball. He fiddles with his grip, aligns his body and aims the club, peering down the fairway several times. He may then even take a practice swing or two before shuffling his feet again and tensing up for the shot. Above all, he has no consistent pre-shot routine.

To give yourself a chance of getting it all right and to develop a sound routine, you could use a simple *aide memoire,* the word GASP. G is for grip, A for aim, S for stance and P for position. In routine, you take your Grip, Aim the club face and align your body in a comfortable Stance with the ball Positioned correctly. Let's look at these essentials in more detail.

First the Grip. Now you seldom see a low handicap golfer (not to mention a pro) with a bad grip. He seems to hold the club firmly, naturally in his hands. But a 'natural' hold for him could seem very uncomfortable and unnatural for you. For there are many ways to hold a club and at least one of them is correct for you, within certain parameters. You must find it and apply it, because if you have been a high handicapper for a number of years and show little sign of improvement, there's a five-to-one chance that your grip is causing your problems and holding you back.

THINK 'GASP' FOR EVERY SHOT.

However, while millions of words have been written by golf instructors on the grip, most of which is good advice, it can be a little confusing for the club golfer. He or she is advised to place the club diagonally across the left palm and keep both palms facing each other, with the 'Vs' of thumbs and forefingers pointing to a spot half way between the nose and the right shoulder – for a neutral grip. The problem is that most golfers do not look at where the 'Vs' point and probably couldn't judge where they were pointing anyway.

For a club golfer, to keep things simple, you will not go too far wrong if you:

- hold the club just above the roots of the fingers of your left hand, so that you see only the thumb and the knuckles of the first two fingers of the hand when your right hand is off the club; and

- when you grip the club with your right hand alone, you see only the nail of your right little finger, but no other finger nails.

From this neutral position, whether you feel more comfy with an overlapping, interlocking or two handed grip (because of the shape of your hands, length of fingers, etc.) it's easy to make it stronger. It doesn't matter which of these grips you use. The great thing is the hands should work together. Golf is a two-handed game and you should feel comfortable. It is important that the grip should be in the bottom of the fingers, not running through the palms.

Beware though that you don't hold the club *entirely* with the fingers. Bob once tried this 'grip' in an effort to get more clubhead speed and distance. He found however that he could not hit the ball consistently in the same direction twice running and abandoned the effort when he started to get blisters.

THE RIGHT GRIP FOR THE RIGHT HAND.

The correct grip for you can only be found with a little experiment, but there can be no variation in the pressure with which you hold the club. It must be firm and light, not squeezed tight. Unfortunately many golfers, judging by the white knuckles and rigid forearms one sees, throttle any chance of a free release out of their swings. You should hold the club lightly at first, for your grip automatically tightens as you accelerate on the downswing. It's rather like driving a nail in with a hammer.

· Next in a sound pre-shot routine comes A for aim and alignment. Forget what you often see on TV, where Greg (and other Tour pros) grounds the club behind the ball, holding only with his right hand, before taking his stance. A pro is concentrating solely on aiming the club in this way; his alignment has become second nature to him, mostly from practice. You however should form your grip firmly on the club and try a practice swing (not taking a divot on the tee) while deciding the line of the shot. To help you line up, choose an aiming point some four or five feet from the ball, a leaf or blade of grass. Then, moving to the ball and looking down on it, you should put the club face behind it squarely along the target line, using your aiming point. To align your body correctly for the shot, just ensure the line of your feet and shoulders are parallel to that line.

Matt, like many club golfers, fails to check this aim, or alignment, of his feet and shoulders with every shot. Then, if his feet point right of the target while his shoulders point left, he develops an ugly shank. It is even more exasperating as Matt doesn't know why it happens, not why it mysteriously disappears (when he aims his body correctly again.) You must *always* check that your body is aimed in line with the clubface for every shot.

With S for Stance, you have to consider where to put your feet, how far apart they should be, your weight distribution, how straight your left arm is at address and how you stand up to the ball.

Feet first. As a club golfer, you should never stand with your feet square to the target line as you swing. They must point *a few degrees* out, otherwise they could lock your backswing and restrict your downswing. They should be as far apart as your normal walking stride, for if too widely spread (as some golfers favour when using a driver) it restricts the hip turn and locks the left knee. This causes a tilt of the shoulders on the backswing, leading to fat shots and slices.

Everything in golf should be 50-50; the tension in both hands, the weight on both legs. Stand evenly balanced. If you start with the preface that everything is 50-50, it makes life much easier.

Your left arm should be stretched out comfortably as you set up and your right elbow relaxed. If you try and force your left arm ramrod stiff (to try and copy the pros in the backswing) your left shoulder will be set too high, impeding a full shoulder turn and probably leading to a reverse pivot.

Standing up to the ball means standing as tall as you can. Don't hunch over; stand up, tilted forward from the *hips* not the waist, with your knees slightly bent. If you bend them too much your backswing will be restricted and you are likely to develop a push or a pushed slice. You must also keep your head up; tucking your chin into your chest causes a short backswing and a steeply angled downswing, causing fat or topped shots. When it's up, there's room for your shoulders to pass beneath. Keep your eyes on the back of the ball and your head still. Look at the ball with both eyes and try not to cock your head on one side. Think that in golf you've got two of everything, use two of everything.

Finally comes P for Position, which decides how you place your body in relation to the ball. Now the club golfer, unless he's seven foot tall and has a very upright swing, should not try to copy the address position of a top pro like Greg Norman, who stands extremely close to the ball, his hands virtually touching his thigh. Norman shifts his body out of the way of his arms Like lightning on his downswing. He's a powerful athlete; the average golfer isn't. So to check if you're standing too close or too far away, you should address the ball and then lower the end of the club's grip until it rests on your left thigh. If it touches about two inches above the kneecap, you're spot on for distance.

As for where the ball should be between the feet, it simply has to sit at the bottom of your normal swing (except for when you are using a driver, when the contact should be on the up). This position for club golfers is about three to four inches inside the left heel (not the two inches used by pros with powerful body actions) and this applies to even the short irons, as the right foot moves nearer to the left when narrowing the stance. The only variation you should consider is when you need to play a lower flying shot, when you should play the ball a little further back, or vice versa for a higher flight.

Comfort Zones

So now you're all set up, feeling positive, balanced, ready to let rip. You aim to swing the club back smoothly . . . but how do you start? Do you waggle? Do you make a forward press? Well, a lazy waggle or two isn't a bad idea, it helps to ease any tension in the arms and

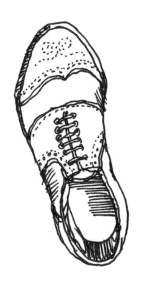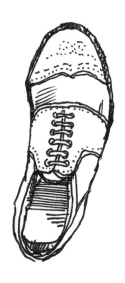

FEET FIRST, FOR AN EASY STANCE.

wrists. A slight forward press by the hands or right knee, or both together, is also quite a good idea, for it's difficult to swing into an easy motion from a static position, a 'dead' start. Most people start with some sort of movement, although a number of the greatest players in the world have had a 'dead' start, namely the most famous doing the rounds at the moment, Seve Ballesteros.

Don't overdo the movement, but when you move the arms gently it does gets things going. Nudging your right knee too much to the left can place too much weight on the left foot, while pressing the hands too far forward can lead to them being in that position at impact which will push the shot off to the right.

This first action leads, almost by recoil, into the takeaway, the initial movement of the club which determines the shape and the rhythm of your swing. For the backswing is just that; a swing. You must swing the club back with your arms, letting your shoulders and hips move in unison against the resistance of a flexed right knee. You must hold your set-up position with a steady head and no swaying, keep your right knee flexed and you must not consciously rotate your forearms or cock your wrists as you start.

When it comes to wrist cock though, the action is very unclear to the club golfer. You see some rolling their wrists, others hooding the club face closed, while many (especially those with a four knuckle grip) seem to yank the club up without moving their arms. None are right and a major cause of this problem is unclear communications, stemming from different swing techniques. Some golf instruction

HOW FAR FROM THE BALL? TOUCH YOUR THIGH.

books and articles today never mention the wrist cock at all. They are written by pros to whom the action is so natural that they cannot understand that the average player is confused by it.

Different descriptions of the cocking action have further confused it totally for the club golfer. Henry Cotton played with the club face working from open to shut. He felt he rolled his wrists on all the full shots, deliberately so in an effort to gain maximum clubhead speed. Sam Snead, the most natural of golfers, said the wrist cock is almost straight up, in line with the forearm. Mr X in the 1970s however advocated hinging the right wrist backwards, square to the plane of the swing, immediately on the takeaway. Nick Faldo also applies this backwards wrist cock as the correct one, when he details how he 'sets his wrists' immediately after the takeaway.

No wonder the poor golfer is confused – and if he thinks too much about the mechanics of the cocking action, it's little wonder if he fails to swing the club at all freely. Happily though, there is a simple way to demonstrate the wrist cock, which should occur as a natural reflex action in response to the motion of the backswing.

First, set up comfortably with your 5-iron, holding the club in a neutral grip. Then separate your hands by about one inch, sliding the right one down the grip. You next swing the club back until its shaft is parallel to the ground – and stop there.

At this point in your swing you should see that the shaft is also parallel to the target line, its butt end level with the ball of your right foot. The toe of the club should point to the sky and the back of your left hand should face straight *forward*. You will also note that your wrists are slightly cocked and they will continue to cock correctly if you swing your arms and turn your shoulders to complete your backswing. A check at the top will show more or less a straight line down the back of your left hand and forearm. That is all there is to cocking correctly – and yes, it is easy to say, though perhaps harder for the club golfer to put into practice.

The position when the club shaft is parallel to the ground (with the toe pointing up) is one you should note in particular. If you can swing through it naturally on your backswing, it means that your club is on plane. It is also the key position that all good golfers reach on the downswing when they start to accelerate through the ball. Whether they loop outwards like Fred Couples before swinging down on the inside, or whether they swing straight back up and down, it is the position their hands, arms and clubs swing through leading to impact (just check a few action stills of players in your favourite golf magazine). So remember this position, look closely at it. Look at how your left hand grips the club, how your right hand sits and how your wrists are cocking naturally.

If however, in that position, the back of your left hand faces the ground, while the clubhead is way outside the line of your feet, you have hooded the club. Conversely, if the back of your hand points to the sky and the clubhead is way inside the line, you have fanned the

Don't let the pros confuse you.

club face open. In both cases, your hands have manipulated the club and you won't be able to cock your wrists properly.

After getting it right, to complete the backswing, you simply continue the swing. Your shoulders should turn away from the ball, the left getting close to your chin when your back will be square to the target. You must not *lift* the club at any stage; you must swing it.

You also have to build some torque into your swing to power it. This is generated by coiling (or pivoting) the body around the axis of the spine and this action is another problem area for the club golfer. He hears or reads that a 'good' pivot means a 90 degree shoulder turn and a 45 degree hip turn. To achieve this he consciously turns his hips, often as much as his shoulders, which builds no torque and simply spins his body around. What you should do is simply concentrate on keeping your right knee flexed at all times when you swing back; that will supply all the torque you might need and keep you balanced in a good position.

As to how far back you should swing, well good golf can be played with very different lengths of backswing. Roland Rafferty and Sandy Lyle, both fine players, don't take the club back as far as the horizontal. On the other hand Payne Stewart takes it well beyond. So, suit yourself, but in fact it's not as easy as that because Doug Sanders would probably have liked to have put 18 inches on the length of his back swing, while Ben Crenshaw would probably like to knock 18 inches off his. So it's not a question of suiting yourself, it's what God has given you – and what he's given you, you stick with and make the most of it. It's knowing 'thyself' that is the most important part sometimes in the game of golf. Bear in mind that while golf is a pleasurable game and you should not force your body into positions where muscular tension is too uncomfortable, you still need torque to swing the club fast and square through the ball.

Swing Reflexology

So far, the swing has been a matter of getting set up right and then swinging the club back smoothly. Now the action speeds up – but there is no need to hurry the downswing consciously. Much of its movement is pure reflex, released from the positive actions that have happened going back.

The first *conscious* action for the club golfer should be to swing his arms down and through the back of the ball, leading with his left forearm.

As you begin that movement, depending on your build, you should feel the muscles of your left side doing much of the work. Your hips will take care of themselves, turning naturally until square to the target by the time you hit the ball. Your shoulders will also turn naturally, and you should make no conscious effort to move them. For timing troubles the club golfer when he tries to swing his body, instead of swinging his arms.

You must realise that while your arms set the plane and the speed of the swing, your body times it and it does this as a reflex action. It is quite easy to demonstrate. Just sit on the edge of a kitchen chair, legs apart and arms extended as if you were about to drive at an imaginary ball. Then swing your arms back, letting your shoulders turn and paying no attention to your legs, and swing down again fast. You'll find that a split second after your arms start down, your legs involuntarily drive to the left. But with reflex action, it's not true that clubhead speed will get distance. If the clubhead is not coming in at the right angle of attack with the body in the right position, you can use your hands as fast as you like and all that you'll get is either one off the heel going away sharply to the left, or a wild slice that travels no more than about 160 yards.

An easy way to see the correct (reflex) use of the hands is to repeat the hands apart half swing you used to check your wrist cock. Only this time swing back a little further until the hands are about waist high, before swinging down and through smoothly. You will find that with your hands separated on the grip, the clubhead will whip through the ball, giving a full release of the hands, arms and right side. And that is the correct way to use your hands in the swing.

Your follow through will take care of itself if you swing easily and in balance; striving for a poised, elegant finish, weight on the left foot, right heel off the ground, gains you little. What counts is a rhythmic swing. Brian found this out to his embarrassment. Stimulated by watching a Pro-Am series on TV during the frozen winter months, he tried to develop a *high* finish to his swing and practised with a walking stick in front of a hall mirror from time to

THE RIGHT WRIST COCK: BACK OF LEFT HAND AND CLUB FACE IN LINE,
FACING FRONT.

time. However . . . when he next played, driving off at the first, Brian found himself peering down the fairway, looking for his ball. His hands were high all right, but the ball was still perched on its tee. Three more airshots in the next two holes convinced him that looks, in golf, were not everything. What you need is a rhythmic swing that hits the ball squarely.

As for tempo, the speed of the backswing is very much an individual matter. Nick Price has a quick rhythm, while Fred

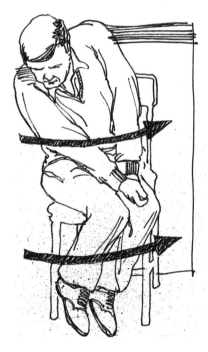

REFLEX ACTION: YOU CAN'T STOP YOUR LEGS KICKING THROUGH.

Couples is slow . . . it's the rhythm they're blessed with! It's the way they walk and it's the way they are. John Jacobs said when playing in strong winds "don't try and hit the ball harder, try and hit it better." Try and keep your balance, try and keep your poise and sweep the ball away. Don't automatically reach for your driver, plan, get yourself in a position to reach the green or get near the green in two. Sam Snead once said if he had to start again he'd only practice driving and shots within a hundred yards of the green; pitches, chipping, bunkers, trouble shots and putting. In other words if he drove well, he'd certainly have a swing that would be able to hit two and three irons and the rest of the game would just fall into place. Good common sense.

But if your driving is amiss, if you slice or hook severely, let's see what we can do to ease those afflictions for the club golfer . . .

REMEDIES FOR SLICE AND HOOK

A dictionary definition of the word 'affliction' is "a state or cause of grievous distress." That definition, for the great majority of club players could equally be applied to the word 'slice'. For more than 80 per cent of all golfers are habitual slicers – and barely one in 50 knows the reason why. It is extraordinary how reasonably intelligent, healthy, well co-ordinated people can be so afflicted. It would seem that slicing is endemic to golf courses and driving ranges worldwide. Little wonder that so many are forever searching for a cure, any cure, that will alleviate their suffering.

The bad news is that there is no panacea. The reason why a ball slices is because the club face is open to the swing line at impact.

The club face stays open for a myriad of reasons. It's all down to the swing line and the approach of the club as it comes into the ball. The set-up plays a big part, the ball position equally so, and then how you move your body throughout the swing also has a very major impact as to where the ball goes.

The good news – is that, while all swings are individual, depending on height, build and age, slicers fall into certain clear categories. If you slice, you're a *ball forward player* or a *body action spinner,* an *upright tilter* or a *reverse pivoter.* You could equally be a *spine jerker,* a *weak swinger,* or a *shoulder shover.* All these are different categories of a slicer and if you have been trying a cure, gleaned from magazines, instruction books or TV, and it hasn't worked, it could be that you've been taking the wrong medicine, trying a cure for a different category to the one you're in.

So let's review the symptoms of the different sufferers, with a suggested treatment for each one. If you can diagnose just how you slice from these examples (and also seek the 'specialist opinion' of your club pro, as you should) then you could alleviate your pernicious slice, forever.

A SLICE COMING UP.

The Wrong Place at the Wrong Time

Just why so many golfers play the ball too far forward in their stance and subsequently slice is hard to determine. It probably comes from their first few rounds as a beginner, when they did not understand the importance of getting their set-up correct, their line-up correct and the ball in the right hittable position. Most people don't stand square to the ball because they feel they're in their own way, so the natural thing for 99 per cent of people who take up golf is to aim left with the ball forward and try and sort of push it away. They have no idea of taking a back swing. People who have played hockey or cricket have some idea of lifting a stick, bat or club to give a ball a whack and that's why most of them make a pretty good fist at golf if they give it a bit of time and effort.

Hitting with the shoulders is also infectious. Golfers have often heard their peers say of a particularly long drive that the striker had "really opened his shoulders on that one". It is a meaningless term, for open shoulders at address can certainly cause a slice, as does hitting with them. In such a case, a player can set up well, with a good grip and make a fluid backswing. At the top, possibly because he freezes, tries to use his shoulders for distance, or locks his swing with a stiff right knee, he starts his downswing with his shoulders. His right one rolls round instead of under, throwing his swing from out to in and his hands are carried through the ball way ahead of the clubhead. Yet another slice results.

The more he slices the more he aims to the left. The more he aims to the left the more he comes across the ball and the more he slices. You can ally that to table tennis or tennis. When you're driving a ball over the net or on a table tennis table, extend your right hand as if you're going to smack somebody across the face and then you take it back. As you hit the ball, the hand rolls over and the palm goes down towards the surface of the table or the ground, which creates a flat shot with a little bit of draw. If you want to slice it, cut it, chop it, the opposite occurs. You take the racket out and across the ball slicing across imparting side spin. That's pretty well the characteristics which are very similar to hooking and slicing at golf and the way the clubhead comes into the ball. If you want to stop slicing (and John Jacobs, the great teacher, once had a proud boast that he could stop anybody slicing within a maximum of a dozen golf balls, perhaps half that number) take a 2-wood, adjust your stance, get the ball in a different position and swing from the inside and then round. Slicing is usually the result of a wood chopping action.

Bob, the stalwart member of our fourball, is a classic example of this category of *ball forward player*. Watch him on the tee. In aiming to the left (which he also does because he has a fuller figure and can thereby see the flag a little more easily) he sets the ball too far forward in his stance. This, with his openly aligned shoulders, effectively weakens his grip. His right hand sits well on top of his left, which has half a knuckle showing, and his arms are stretched out and rigid. His right shoulder is too high as well.

As a result, when Bob starts his takeaway, he has to fight taking the club straight back. So he pulls his arms inside on too flat a plane, rolling the club face open. At the top his body recoil shoves his right shoulder out, throwing his arms in a steep out to in swingpath. Coupled with his weakened grip, the ball flies off left before curling right, although maddeningly the odd one keeps on going straight left, as do his short irons.

At least, given this shot pattern, Bob can manage to play a round breaking 100, scoring less if he aims left with his longer clubs instead of stubbornly pointing down the middle. But how much better it would be if he hit through the ball with the club face square to the target when he was aligned square to it himself. To achieve this there is a simple cure – although knowing it and applying it are two different things. All Bob has to do is to understand *why* he is slicing. Then he has to set the ball further back in his stance (three inches inside his left heel) when his club face, shoulders and feet are square to the target line. This will have the effect of naturally strengthening his grip. Finally, he has to get out of the habit of rolling, or fanning, his club on the takeaway and swing back without manipulating it with his hands.

You too have to take this medicine if you're a ball forward player – and it can be very difficult to swallow. When you are correctly lined up to swing your club back on an inside path and then down along the target line, you will probably feel decidedly uncomfortable (particularly if you've sliced most of your golfing life). It will seem

WHEN THE BALL IS TOO FAR FORWARD, THE RIGHT SHOULDER MOVES
OUT AND OVER.

that you are about to compound your slice by hitting the ball out to the right. Yet you have to find out that you can swing from the inside out to the right to hit the ball straight. So head for the practice ground (just for once) and set up square. Before you hit any balls, place a club between your feet and the ball position, angled a few degrees right of your target line. If you swing back parallel with its shaft, you'll be on a natural inside path. Forget your anxiety. Just keep your eye on the back of the ball, swing back along the shaft line and . . . watch the result.

There's another drill you can try out to help you swing back correctly, although it's quite difficult to control at first, so watch out for anyone standing nearby. Simply hit some balls using your right arm only, teed up off your right heel. Use your 8-iron and set up square. You will find that your right shoulder will be lower at address and you will swing from inside to along the target line. It can pay dividends in ironing out that left to right flight.

The *body action spinner* also needs advice to cure the same distressing shot pattern. To diagnose his condition, he should note that while he mostly slices, some of his shots are skied high, while the occasional one dribbles along the fairway to the left.

There's nothing usually wrong with his ball position, set-up, takeaway or backswing. The trouble comes in the downswing – and what causes the complaint is probably all in the mind. Maybe he tries too hard to 'start the downswing with a turn of the left hip'. Or perhaps, particularly if he is a senior golfer, he strives for the 'late hit' position so encouraged in the teaching of the 1950s and '60s. Or he could have been admonished before, having dug several deep divots, that he was 'casting his hands from the top'.

Whatever the primary cause, his downswing is bodged. Sliding and spinning his hips too soon, he seems to be trying to hit the ball with his body, as his arms swing down too late. If he grips too tightly to stop casting, he also locks his hands and arms which, given his excessive body spin, throws his right shoulder out and the club comes down on a steep out to in path.

If you are in this category of slicer you will have to learn to stop swinging yourself instead of the club. The specific is to practice swinging with legs and feet touching. Tee up the ball, use a five or six iron and simply swing the club up and down with the arms. You will have to anyway. If you try and force the swing with conscious hip or leg action, or power it with your shoulders, you will immediately lose your balance. You won't be able to swing too fast either.

If you find that you are throttling the club involuntarily, and not getting enough swish as you hit the ball, make a series of half swings with the hands apart on the grip. You'll see the club flash through the hitting area and condition yourself to a free release of the hands. You should not be surprised when you start striking the ball squarely, sending it soaring straight on line (if it doesn't, check your alignment). But you will be surprised at the distance you get from the feet together swing. It will only be some ten yards shorter than your best efforts from your normal swing. Hopefully, when you've applied the specific, your best efforts will become your norm.

The Reverse Pivot

The *upright tilter* is another category of slicer which is common among club golfers. Now rocking and tilting the right shoulder upwards on the backswing, rather than letting it turn away naturally, is a fault that can also develop in the swings of a number of good golfers, including probably the greatest of all time, Jack Nicklaus. He has spoken and written openly about his affliction, which he took positive steps to cure in 1980.

Jack always strived for a long, high flying shot, which demanded a big, high swing arc. But in his early days his very upright swing was also 'deep' (the club at the top being above or even behind his right shoulder) for he had a very strong coil. Then his backswing gradually changed for a number of reasons, possibly through playing in windier conditions in Florida. It stayed steep, but lost its depth. He didn't coil fully, for the more directly upwards the arms swing, the sooner the body stops coiling. Also the more upright the swing, the steeper the downswing and the harder it is to hit the ball squarely.

As a result, Jack suffered from a feeling of hitting the ball badly, obliquely, and he lost distance. But with his considerable ability and experience, he could still control the ball sufficiently despite the affliction. He could still think his way around a golf course, he could certainly still putt and he could still win. This is not the case for the average golfer who is an upright tilter; mostly all he can do is slice.

Matt, the tallest, youngest member of our fourball, is a prime example. Most of his long shots start off straightish before swinging right and he often thins shots, although he occasionally hits one fat. The root cause of this is bad posture. Matt sets up with his back and neck bent too far forwards over the ball, possibly determined to 'keep his head down'. Now the more inclined he is at address, the more his shoulders (and hips) will rock and tilt upwards, rather than turn, on the backswing. This, subsequently, causes a slide and blocks the body coming down. The left side doesn't clear and this forces the club into a steep downwards arc in which the hands and arms can't square the club face in time.

Jack Nicklaus' cure would also work for Matt. First, Jack started to stand much taller to the ball, setting up with his back more upright and his head up. When he began to address the ball in this way, he said that he felt uncomfortable (like, he imagined, many golfers who slice feel most of the time). But this taller posture allowed his right shoulder to turn properly and his body to clear as he swung through.

Another element in his cure (which might not be applicable to all upright tilters) was to set up with his head more in the centre of his stance. Previously he used to address the ball with his head 'back', much nearer his right side, to ensure against it being pulled forwards

AN UPRIGHT TILTER, WEIGHT ON THE LEFT.

by his strong leg drive. His more centred head made it easier for him to swing back on an inside path, as did the final element of his cure, letting his right elbow fold earlier on the backswing. If you are an upright tilter, you might try the same prescription; if it worked for Jack, it could work for you.

Over-upright, uncoiled swings are also the symptoms of another category of slicer: the *reverse pivoter*. Here the sufferer finds himself leaning to the left at the top and he then falls back onto his right foot as he swings down, losing distance and often slicing severely. Diagnosing the affliction is easy; you'll find yourself leaning left at the top, then as you 'fire and fall back' your right foot will be flat on the ground. But the causes of this are several, as are the cures, which concern the set-up (again) of hands, arms and head.

First, and perhaps rather obviously (though not to him) is the golfer who sets up with much of his weight on his left side. He may well not do this deliberately: it can stem from a strong grip with the hands several inches ahead of the ball. From that position, he can only swing the club straight back, with little turn as the weight stays left, which forces his weight right coming down. The cure is easy. He should check his set-up and ensure that he's evenly balanced, with his hands just ahead of (or hovering over) the ball.

Over active hands though can cause a reverse pivot, even if your set-up is OK. When hands are too active in the takeaway they can push the clubhead way outside the target line, which means that you swing too steeply. To cure this variation, firm up your grip to quiet your hand action and concentrate on swinging your arms away. Check that when the shaft of the club is parallel to the ground it is also parallel to the target line. That way you'll be on plane for a good shot.

Arms, particularly the left one, can also lead to the reverse pivot. They should certainly not be too rigid as you set up: they should dangle in a firm, yet relaxed way. However if your left arm gets too relaxed and if you let it *bend* too much on the backswing, you'll be too upright, won't coil properly and will reverse pivot. The cure is to swing back the left arm as straight as you can without straining, deliberately trying to swing flatter, until your weight shifts naturally right at the top. When it does that, it will move automatically left coming down.

Finally, for certain reverse pivoters, it all comes to the head. Practically every golfer has been told firmly at some time to keep his head still. Some have also been instructed not to sway as they swing (despite the example of Curtis Strange, whose different, yet effective technique won him two US Opens). However, while coiling, not swaying, around a steady spine and head is fundamental to good golf, some golfers carry the still head position to an extreme.

Rigidly holding their heads immobile, they tense up their bodies and their arms and swing back into . . . a reverse pivot. The prescription? Forget about the head. Let it move slightly to the right going back if it wants to. Just concentrate on swinging smoothly and the head will take care of itself.

Spine Jerkers and Others

Posture is clearly very important for good golf. A top pro always looks balanced over the ball, leaning forward from his hips, knees flexed, arms extended, with his back (and spine) at an angle of some 30 degrees to the vertical. Moreover, during his swing through impact, this angle of inclination does not change. This is not the case with many golfers, who are afflicted with a jerky movement in the downswing, dipping or lifting their spines, which can cause an out to in swing and a slice.

If you are such a *spine jerker*, bad posture is the prime cause – and there is also a good chance that you're a little shorter than average height, or on the other hand a lot taller. The shorter golfer can get into bad habits by bending his knees too much at address. He sets up with too upright a spine angle (say 15 degrees) his feet spread wide and his weight back on his heels. As his weight shifts naturally further backwards at the top, he tends to jerk forward on the downswing, dipping his spine and scything out to in. His cure is to get his posture right from the start. He must bend more from the hips, with less flex in his knees, a narrower stance and his weight over the balls of his feet. He may feel too close to the ball to start with, but the results of straighter shots should soon convince him that the medicine is working.

Tall golfers who tend to lift their spines as they swing have exactly the opposite symptoms. Possibly in an effort to stop feeling they are stretching out for the ball, they often set up bent too far forwards (with a spine angle of say 40 degrees). This is not like Matt's crouching stance, for he was well balanced. In this case, the golfer tends to have a narrow stance, his knees are not flexed enough and his weight is forward on his toes.

As a result, to keep balanced on the back swing, he jerks his spine, which leads to his slice. Once again, he has to treat his posture. He needs to stand more upright with a slightly wider stance and well flexed knees. At first, he may tend to top the ball, but after a while his timing will improve and his slice should fade away.

Physique, your physique, can also be a cause of your slice. It's not just a question of being short or tall, where the problem is really bad posture, it's whether you are slightly built or have a much fuller figure. Both can be contributory factors, but neither need lead to a permanent affliction.

The slightly built golfer who does not have much strength in hands or wrists is often a *weak swinger*. He (or she, as many senior ladies come in this category) tends to stand upright and swing upright too, to ease the physical pressure on stomach and hands. As a result he doesn't coil in the backswing and comes down on a steep out to in path, while his weak hand action ensures a short, high slice.

Such a swinger has to develop a more rotary swing and if he cannot physically swish through the ball any quicker, he must try at least to square the clubhead at impact. One treatment is to ensure that he plays with lightweight clubs and sets up less upright (like the shorter player) with less flex in the knees and the weight further forward. After takeaway, he must make an effort to cock the wrists fully before swinging the arms down on the inside.

A slight change of grip could also help to speed up hand action. This is the medicine prescribed for Brian, the slightest, senior member of our fourball. While not swinging too upright (because he strives for a draw for distance and so sets up closed and swings back quite flat) he has a weak hand action which sends the ball off right of target, to curve further right. Brian (and many others) should realise that it would be far better for them to adopt a strong grip. Many top women pros use a three knuckle grip very effectively, as they know they lack sheer strength. As weak swingers also tend to grab the club too tightly to raise it, which locks the wrists, Brian should also ease up on his grip pressure, especially with his right hand.

The bulky golfer equally has got a problem when it comes to coiling properly on the backswing. If you are a heavyweight with a large chest and waist and muscular arms, you could well belong to the last (but not least) category of slicer: the *shoulder shover*. If you are such a swinger, it's simply because you're not too supple and you find it hard to turn your shoulders sufficiently. As a result, you swing back very flat (the most common fault among the heavies) from an open stance (which you probably adopted to see where you are trying to hit the ball). Now because your arms finished the backswing moving

TOO STEEP AN ARC FOR A WEAK SWINGER.

around rather than up, they recoil into the downswing moving out and you shove with your shoulders to get some power into the shot. So you tend to hit it short, left to right, pulling your short irons and occasionally shanking one.

But don't despair. Some sterling heavyweights (Billy Caspar and Craig Stadler to name a formidable duo) have amply demonstrated that extra poundage does not restrict good golf. First, you will have to guard against setting up open: particularly with your build, it restricts the backswing, so set up slightly closed. Then you must bend over more from the hips, taking care not to have too much weight forward on your toes. This will promote a fuller wind up (standing closed) and a more upright swing (bending forward) as your shoulders will tilt more on the backswing.

You need to swing back slowly. But how far back? The fact is that your natural instincts will tell you how far to go. Some people will always have too long a swing, some people will always struggle to get to the horizontal. There is nothing wrong with a three-quarter backswing, which could suit many golfers who only play on weekends. You could combine it with a stronger grip, swing your arms down fast, aim for a high finish . . . and you could soon be hitting a long, controlled draw.

As you are easing your affliction (hopefully taking your medicine out on the practice ground) you will, as a confirmed golfer, still want to play. When you tee up though, do remember that curing a deep rooted affliction takes time. So use your head and give yourself a chance with the long shots. Tee your ball up high on the right of the tee and aim towards the left side of the fairway. Then at least you should be in play if the odd shot curls right. If others curve in the opposite direction, as they very well could, it will make a change searching for them in the left light rough.

Hook as You Stand

These teeing up tactics won't do at all however for the hookers of the world. This minority group suffers in many ways from a more pernicious affliction, as the ball that swings hard left is generally hit a lot harder and runs even deeper into trouble. Hookers also don't fall into such interesting categories as slicers, as there are basically only three reasons why they hook – and one can lead to the others. But first of all let's dispose of one misconception: anyone who hits the ball left of target, for it to spin further left, is not a hooker. He is a puller, with a slicer's out to in swing, who has simply closed the club face through the ball. The true hook stems from a closed club face it's true, but the swing path is from in to out, or in to along the target line.

Unlike the slicer, the hooker has no problems in swinging his arms down fast. Quite the reverse. His grip however can cause the problem. If your shots start out straight before hooking, especially if they fly low (so low, you tend to leave your driver in the bag) then you almost certainly have the wrong grip for your swing. It could be too strong, which you can easily check by swinging back to the shaft parallel position. Even if the club is aligned along the target line and its toe points up, if the back of your left hand, or the palm of your right, faces the sky, you're too strong.

You may also be gripping too lightly with your right hand. Now while a weak left wrist through impact can let the strong right hand roll over it, closing the club face, an overtight left hand grip can slow the butt of the club in the hitting area. A light right hand grip in combination (which makes the right wrist more flexible and active) can whip the club face closed, so you hook. Getting the grip pressure all right isn't easy. You can check its neutrality, but if you still suffer, try holding the club a little more in the palms of your hands. Thicker than standard grips could help you to do this.

The fact remains that it is easier to use clubs with loft; the easiest of all are the five, six and seven irons. Why? Because they're short in shaft and have plenty of loft. A driver, a one and two iron are the most difficult because they're the longest in shaft and with the least amount of loft. So it's very important to think and use the clubs at your disposal. Remember Bobby Locke, one of the greatest pound for pound players ever, drove with a club with a fair amount of loft on it, almost a 2-wood. He had a number one head cover on it, but that was just to fool the opposition. Peter Thomson won certainly two or three of his Open championships using a 3-wood off the tee. Why? Because the seaside links courses, the championship courses, were hard, fast, bouncy, runny and the drive was only a positional shot setting up the next stroke to the green. He knew he had to be on the fairway from the tee otherwise he was a 'dead duck', so he settled on a slightly shorter distance from the tee although the hardness of the ground and the run of the ball took him well above the average length a professional drives and he was one of the world's great players.

So many handicap players persist with a driver when they should think twice. They read articles extolling the virtues of certain clubs and having spent a lot of money buying one they are loathe not to use it. In fact they would do far better to use a club with loft because the great thing is to get the ball on the fairway then you can start to play golf. Driving has to be closely behind putting as the most important element in the game; or so we believe.

With cause and effect at work, many hookers like Doug in our fourball are just not prepared to change anything. Doug, who has a *very* strong grip, has tried different holds in the past but couldn't stick with any of them because it felt too uncomfortable. As a result, he (like others) aims right of target instinctively to stop the ball going left. This closed stance sets the ball too far back in the stance, which makes him swing too far inside and too flat. If the club face is square to the target, his long shots will fly right to left, while his medium irons are usually pushed straight out right. He is quite philosophical about it all, but his game could improve a great deal with just a little common sense.

Doug has to set up square, with the ball further forward in his stance. He can check his alignment and its results on the

GRIP, AIM AND THIS POSITION = HOOK.

practice ground before his next round. If he's on his own, he could place a club parallel to the target line and stand with his toes almost touching it. This would help to alleviate his very inside backswing, but he really also has to weaken his grip a little to straighten things out.

The third cause of the dreaded hook, which often develops from a very inside backswing, is when the body gets in the way of the arms as they swing down. As the body does not clear (perhaps because it does not coil enough on the backswing) the arms are blocked and the wrists unhinge and rotate rapidly through impact, closing the club face.

This 'body in the way' condition can sometimes be caused deliberately by golfers who exaggerate the concept of hitting against a firm left side. It can also come from setting up closed, as the golfer feels he has already half completed his backswing and so does not fully turn his shoulders, which inhibits the turn of the left hip. More often though the position of the feet are the culprits.

If your left side feels over rigid through impact, check your feet. You could unwittingly have set up with a square left foot, while your right points well right, making your coil easier but building little torque. In addition, coming down, your left foot will stop your body clearing, stiffening the left side and blocking a free arm swing. Far better to point the left foot out a little down the fairway, clearing the way for a long, straight shot towards the flat.

THE EASY APPROACH

F ew club golfers can ever hope to match their local pro with a long shot off the tee, 250 yards plus down the middle, though many bust a gut trying to emulate him on every drive. Once in several attempts, it's true, they do get off a pretty good 'un (usually when thinking about things other than golf) but by and large few are really confident on the tee.

Most however find the second shot on the short par fours a great deal easier. With the mid irons, the four, five and six, the swing is more compact, there is greater control and hence higher confidence. Overall, the swing is a little more upright than with the woods, sweeping the arms firmly down from a three quarter backswing and always taking enough club.

The biggest difference between the high handicapper and the low is this shot to the green. Most often, the former presses, flays away trying to power a six iron 160 yards and pulling into trouble, rather than hitting a crisp five. With these mid irons, you have to swing well within yourself, playing carefully away from trouble, aiming safely for the centre of the green, well clear of bunkers or surrounding bushes or trees at the back. Look once, look twice at the distance, and then pick a big enough club to get you there.

CHECK ALL THE PENALTIES BEFORE YOU HIT AN APPROACH.

From around 100 yards out though you don't always go for the pin. You've got to sum up where the flag is positioned on the green. What are the penalties if you miss on the wrong side? Is there a bunker? Is there an abyss? Does it drop into the sea? All sorts of things come into consideration for the handicap player. It would be great to see a golf tournament played where the caddies are not allowed to pace the course, things have to be judged by eye and there are no flags in the greens. In other words, you hit the fairway and then you judge whether it's a 7- or a 9-iron and you aim at the green. Your short irons (the 7-, 8- and 9-) are the *scoring* clubs. You'd be amazed how many balls finish stone dead and most likely the standard of play could easily improve because too many pros are misguided enough to think you must go at the pin, you must attack, you must attack. That's all well and good, but you must also know when to defend, which is equally as important.

This distance out (from 130-160 yards) is a hard one for the golfer to judge and control, as they can call for many half and three quarter swings. The feel of each varying from player to player. In one case, Bob might take a half swing with a 7-iron, while Doug could take a three quarter swing with an eight. Less than full shots however are never easy for the club golfer to execute. Often a semi-backswing jerks down in an effort to hit the ball harder: more often, an overswing leads to a deceleration on the way down.

So go for a full shot whenever you can, by doing what few club golfers do, going down the grip if the distance is shorter than your chosen club. As a guide, every inch lower that you grip from the top of the club cuts its range by some fifteen yards, given a full backswing. But even hitting flat out, take note: the average golfer cannot hit his pitching wedge 100 yards. Unless he thins one, the best he can manage is about 90. He can also only hit his sand wedge some 65 yards, which is why so many bury their balls in forward placed greenside bunkers.

Making a Pitch

All these shots are played with a 'normal' swing, where the wrists come in automatically at impact, the right hand gradually rolling over the left into the follow through. From 50 yards out however, it all changes and you have to use a true pitching action to loft the ball over bunkers or water, so that it lands softly and trickles up to within a couple of yards of the flag.

Now you may feel you have heard or read a great deal about pitching, as nearly every golf magazine carries many articles by Tour pros on the subject. But if you're still not getting it close (or if you stub, jab, flip or scoop your pitches, as Doug in our fourball is wont to) pay heed, for you should appreciate the *why* of pitching as well as the wherefore.

The first consideration is the club to use. Now with a pitch you are trying to maximise backspin, which means using the most lofted club in your bag, normally your sand iron. Pitching wedges have a loft of 48–52 degrees, while sand irons vary between 54–58 degrees. (The third, or lob wedge, carried by top pros like John Daly, which has a loft of 60–64 degrees is a relatively new concept.) But many golfers are afraid to use their sand irons for pitching (after all, what's a *pitching* wedge for?)

One reason is that the leading edge of the sand iron often seems more than slightly off the ground, particularly if the club has a generous bounce sole. Players like Doug who thins every time he tries it, prefer the pitching wedge as its leading edge is its lowest point. This can, however, dig into the ground on a short shot causing a fluff. So the best counsel is to learn how to use your sand iron for all pitches from 50 yards out.

But what do you pitch at? Not the flag directly, as almost all pitches by club golfers have some forward roll, never screwing back like those of the Tour pros. So you have to pick a landing area on the green with care, watching the slopes, and mind you don't foreshorten the distance to the flag. It's easy to think you are aiming 10 feet short, only to find the ball lands 10 feet shorter than that. As for the amount of forward roll you get, this obviously depends on how high you hit the ball, or whether you're playing from the rough, but remember also to note if the green is sloping downhill away from you, or uphill. With a good lie to a level green though, you should manage to limit the roll to some seven to ten feet with a 50 yard pitch.

Aiming where you want to hit it is another consideration and major problem for many golfers. Bob is one such. He has heard, rightly, that you pitch with an arm swing and use little body action, so to give room for the arms to swing he stands open to the target line. The trouble comes when he aligns his shoulders open with his feet, even though the club face is square. As a result, in trying to swing back normally, he pulls the club inside and coming down throws it outside, pulling the ball left and into trouble. He has to learn to keep his shoulders square to the line when he pitches, though if he opened his stance a little it would do no harm.

So now for the true pitching action from some 50 yards out. You should set up with a narrow, slightly open stance, evenly balanced with the ball between your feet (not back towards the right, as you would probably thin it). You will also be gripping the club about one inch down from the top, depending on how far you generally hit it. What you do not want to do next is take a long easy swing back and decelerate down, as your right hand would flip the clubhead through and you'll fluff.

Instead you swing back about half way, letting your wrists cock fully. Keep it slow and as you swing down through the ball let your right hand release against a firm, guiding left hand. The right must not roll over the left through impact or even in the follow through. It stays *under* the club. You do not scoop the ball; you hit down firmly and with this pitching action the club face points to the sky at the end of the follow through, which should just about equal the backswing in length.

A TRUE PITCHING ACTION.

The Gentle Roll

The pitching action is identical for shots from 25 yards out. With a full grip, you would probably swing back until the club shaft was just past parallel to the ground. Feeling the amount of swing though for medium to short pitches is quite difficult. To enhance it, you could bowl a few balls underarm with your right hand (on a practice green). Aim for a target area some yards short of the flag and bowl a series of balls from a variety of distances until you start to group them closely near the hole. Now try the same series with your sand iron. The feel you get for each shot in your right hand is the same as when you are bowling with it. The action of your right hand is the same and this easy movement can be used to assess the shot when you are about to play one 'for real' on the course (only don't take too many practice bowls, please).

At 10 yards out, feel generally seems to desert the club golfer. Either he swings back too far and decelerates down, thinning the ball weakly, or worse still he sockets. This dreaded shot happens because he has heard he should open the club face and play a little cut shot, so that the ball lands lightly. In so doing, particularly without a lot of practice, it is easy to hit the ball with the neck of the club. So the club golfer should avoid unnecessary cut shots and he should neither thin nor socket if he uses the right technique.

It's an extraordinary thing, but a fact, that Arnold Palmer was one of the world's greatest chippers and for his standard of play one

IMAGINE BOWLING TOWARDS THE FLAG BEFORE YOU PITCH.

of the worlds worst pitchers of the ball. The same could be said for Jack Nicklaus. He was never a great chipper or pitcher or indeed bunker player, but he got by with probably the most clinical golfing brain ever and the ability to harness his power and think clearly in moments of great stress. He was also a wonderful 'holer-out': from anything from four to ten feet – Nicklaus reigned supreme. If you analyse Nicklaus' game, the most successful player the world has ever seen by a distance, it's very hard to say what he was best at. Some people would say a 1- or 2-iron, some people say his putting, some would say his power, but nothing actually stood out like, shall we say, Gary Player's bunker play, Bobby Locke's putting, Sam Snead's swing, or Hogan's shot making ability. The fact remains that Nicklaus had the ability, he had all these bits and pieces of ingredients that looked quite innocuous if you took them bit by bit – but put them all together and you had a wonderful golfing machine.

The short pitch should be played with firm (not rigid) arms and wrists. You should hold the club a couple of inches down from the top of the grip (straightening the line of arms and wrists) with its shaft absolutely vertical in the middle of your stance, so that the club face shows its maximum loft.

The swing is a short, crisp, pendulum action, with no wrist break. The club face is hooded on the backswing, which travels only some three feet for a ten yard pitch. At impact, the sole of the sand iron 'bounces' down behind and slightly beneath the ball, just denting the ground, but never cutting in with the leading edge. With this contact, the full loft of the club pops the ball up softly. Through impact there is still no breaking or turning of the wrists and with the right hand staying under the grip, the club face looks at the sky when it reaches knee height.

Summarising it simply: the short pitch is a neat, brushing swing, where the club face moves from shut to open, producing lots of backspin without having to play a wristy, or cut shot. The difficulty for some golfers is to avoid a jerky movement and to keep the legs passive, rather than rigid. Some also tend to hit the ball too firmly, having 'dead' instead of 'soft' hands.

This term 'soft hands' was often used to describe players with a very good short game – and one of the best short game players in the world, Mark McNulty, practices what he preaches when it comes to the short pitch. To have the ball come off the club face softer than normal and avoid hitting it too firmly, he uses a reverse overlap grip, with his left forefinger riding on the little finger of his right hand. This reduces the hand action in his short pitching and keeps his wrists firm, something that every golfer should attempt.

Chips Anyone?

The reverse overlap grip is also used for chipping – and the short chip from a few feet off the green, with about ten yards to the flag, is one of the most important shots for scoring. You need to minimise

JIGGER

backspin with this shot, just lofting the ball onto the green so that it can roll at least two thirds of the way to the hole.

Most golfers can gauge roll better than flight, so you should always play a short chip when you can (when there are no hazards other than thick wet grass between you and the green). The choice of club is also important. Some top pros recommend using the five, six, seven, eight and nine irons for different short chips, believing that there is an ideal club for every combination of flight and roll. There is, but this makes things too complicated for the club golfer. It is better to become very familiar with just one club and learn how to use it with some confidence.

For those who watch golf on the TV, you've probably noticed how many of the top players chip with a very lofted club – a nine, a wedge or even a sand iron. They move the weight onto the left side, the hands go forward, the blade of the club is squared up and the ball is struck sharply and firmly. Because the face is closed, the trajectory is low, but it's running, spinning and slowing down; it's under control, it's not running free and over the years this has become a way of playing the short shots. Years ago people used to take a 4-iron to play a running chip from off the green and very rarely was a lofted club used, because that appeared to be the most difficult shot. It's not any more. Those who chip poorly may well be induced into trying a runner-up, or a 'jigger' as it was called years ago. A jigger is a wide bottomed club with the loft of a four or five iron with a shorter shaft and the club is played pretty well like a long put. Again timing is very important. If you're too quick and too short in the back swing you'll top it or hit the ground behind; it's very important to get the right sort of tempo.

The 7-iron is normally the right club for the average golfer. It should carry about a third of the distance of a shot, letting the ball roll for the remainder. Its lie however is not upright enough ideally. To explain: a typical mistake of club golfers is to play the ball too far from their feet, which leads to many pushed or pulled chips as the clubhead swings across the target line. They reach for the ball and so have to manipulate the club face on the downswing – and they further push the ball if they play it too far back in their stance. So you have to play the ball close in to get a more straight back, straight through swing path: very akin to the action of a putt.

You should set up with the ball some ten inches from your feet, with your eyes directly over it. To do this, many golfers would find that a specialised chipping club, with the loft of a 7-iron and an upright lie, would pay for itself quickly. Many a senior golfer wielding such a club has won more than the odd ball from its judicious use. It's good for long pitches (from some 50 yards out) and it's a handy club to have in the bag if you need to play a shot left handed, as its back has the same loft as its face.

If you only have your trusty 7-iron however, you will need to sit it a little on its toe to keep the shaft as upright as possible. Using the reverse overlap grip, hold it some three inches from the top and swing back a few feet (*not* trying to hood the clubface). As with a long putt, the arms and club should work together, with a little 'give' in the wrists and legs to avoid a jerky action. At impact and beyond, the clubhead must not overtake the hands. How firmly do you strike the ball? Well, do study the grain on the green before chipping. If it's with you, you will get more roll. If against, the ball will pull up more quickly and you'll need a firmer swing.

Some golfers cannot judge this strike easily and can even get the equivalent of the putting 'yips' with their short chips. Brian from our fourball is one. He duffs some, thins others and occasionally double hits. Part of the reason is poor technique, but a major part is a growing lack of confidence – and once this happens to your chipping, it can run rampant through the rest of your game.

The same thing happened to Peter Senior, that gifted Australian Tour pro, with the 'shouldery', though effective swing. For no apparent reason he suddenly started to yip his short chips so badly that he sometimes even missed the ball. He felt it was possibly because he had too much flex in his wrists, which became uncontrollable. Senior's cure was to adopt a method which would suit Brian and others who tend to lack confidence with their chips. He started to use a 'cack handed' or 'cross handed' grip: where the right hand was above the left, with no fingers overlapping, and both thumbs were down the shaft, palms opposing.

This grip, he felt, locked his left wrist so that it would not collapse at impact. Then all he had to do was to swing his left arm down the target line and the club face had to stay square. Keeping his hands ahead of the clubhead, swinging through to a follow through the same length as his backswing, gave him confidence that he could repeat the shot consistently. Even though the grip looks a little ungainly, if you've got any problems with your short chips, why not try it?

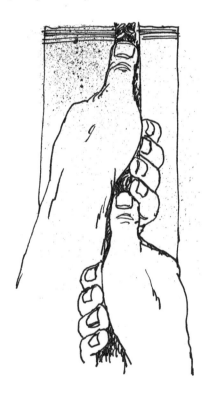

THE CROSS HAND GRIP: NO OVERLAP, THUMBS DOWN SHAFT.

You should also be quite prepared to try the putter from off the fringe. Dave Thomas who tied Peter Thomson in the Open at Royal Lytham, only to lose in the play-off, was an expert at this shot. A poor chipper, he always used his putter from off the green and developed a wonderful touch with it. So, for the club golfer, even if you are four or five feet from the green, if the grass between you and the edge is short and dry and the ground is flat, you can be as successful putting off the green as on it. Remember the putt is the simplest shot to play under such favourable conditions and the easiest to control. It will never get you into serious trouble. It may run off line, bobbling and bouncing off worm casts, but you are not likely to top the ball or hit behind it.

Even if the lie is bare or the ball is in a scuff mark, the putter could be the club. You also don't have to hit under the ball, just make contact with the back of it – and it may even be the best way of running over a bank or up to the top level of a two tier green. So don't feel it is *infra dig* to use your putter off the green. After all, the object of the exercise is simply to get it close . . .

ESCAPE FROM THE SAND

Many golfers seem to feel that there are thousands of redundant, unnecessary bunkers scattered across courses throughout the world. They cost too much money to maintain (for the sand, greenkeeper's time, etc) and serve mostly the 'burrowing animals'. They also seem to lurk along fairways not just to penalise the bad shot, but often to grab up the near good one as well.

With this attitude, it's not surprising that club golfers generally are a little afraid of getting into a bunker. They are also weary of being told, by people who should know better, that the sand recovery shot is one of the simplest in golf, because it has a great margin for error. That margin causes golfers world wide to excavate enough sand every month to cover the Pyramids.

All the members of our fourball actively dislike bunkers, Bob not least. For despite having spent quite a bit of time erasing his footprints in them, he still does not use any common sense, or try to apply any basic technique, when his ball ends up 'on the beach'.

Take the long sixteenth. Having ended up in a fairway bunker on the right, some 230 yards from the green, Bob carefully selects his three wood. The lip, he thinks, is quite shallow, but he ignores the fact that his ball is sitting a little down in the sand. Swinging hard, to get the distance, he tops it about ten feet forward, still in the bunker.

Worse is to follow. Three shots later, he lands in a bunker by the green, about twenty yards from the flag. This time he does take his sand iron, but when he's standing over the ball he starts to have doubts. On the one hand, he's afraid that if he takes too little sand he could skim the ball over the green. On the other, if he took too much (as he often does) he might just about flop it out, if he was lucky. In the end, as the bunker isn't all that deep, he decides to chip it cleanly off the surface, taking no sand at all. The result is almost inevitable. His tentative swing catches the ball a little heavy, sending it to the lip before it rolls back into one of his footprints. His second effort, very much harder, with a closed club face, digs the club deep and the ball doesn't even reach the lip this time.

Taking three out of a bunker is bad for anyone's blood pressure, so let's see how Bob could have played the hole (as any sensible golfer should have, given that he somehow managed to get into both bunkers along the way).

Sweeping the Long Shots

With long bunker shots, you don't want to get the ball too far back in your stance because you're taking loft off the club and you're driving into the ground. One of the best players of long bunker shots ever was Eric Brown. He could get a 4-iron to a bunker shot where normal human beings would be thinking eight or a nine iron maximum, but he was able to open the face, as indeed Ballesteros does, and accelerate through and get elevation by just plucking the ball off the top of the sand. Remember, it's rather like taking a driver off the fairway, if there's nothing in your way and you strike the ball right on the equator, you sweep it away. Providing the club is sweeping in along the level of the fairway the same as in the bunker, you pick the ball up and away it'll go. As long as you don't hit the ball above the equator, if it's in the right position and the hands are moving the clubhead through the ball at a fast rate, the ball should come out and go well down the fairway.

Facing a long shot from a fairway bunker, the last club a golfer like Bob should pick is his 3-wood. He is not Seve Ballesteros. Even given a good lie on the sand, the 'biggest' club he should consider is his 4-iron, but before he selects any club, he should first examine the lie, because if the ball is sitting down in the sand at all, he can't hope to get any distance on his shot, and so should just play the ball out onto the fairway.

Next he should look closely at the lip of the bunker between him and the distant green. How high is it, in relation to where the ball lies? Could he get a four or five iron up quickly enough to clear it? Then, and only then, should he select a club – and he should be sure that it has plenty of loft to spare to clear the bunker. With 230 yards to go, he is far better off playing a 5-iron and then a full pitching wedge to the green rather than flaying away trying to get close. He would be hard pressed anyway getting there with his 3-wood from a good lie on the fairway. So the 5-iron would probably be the right club.

USE COMMON SENSE IN THE SAND, NOT A WOOD.

In the bunker, Bob should set up to the ball with a shoulder-width stance and make certain that his feet were firmly anchored in the sand. To allow for lowering the base of his stance by this inch or so, he then has to grip fairly firmly a bit down the club. The ball should be positioned perhaps just a little back in his stance, but this should be square to the target line, as if he was playing a normal fairway shot.

His swing should be 'normal' as well; that is to say he should make a three quarters backswing and sweep the club down on a shallow arc, avoiding a steep, chopping action at all costs. But he should swing a little slower than usual, for he has to be sure that he contacts the ball without taking a single grain of sand. A good tip in this respect is to *aim* to hit the top half of the ball: Bob should watch his intended impact point on the back of it closely as he swings down.

In this way, he's far more likely to pick the ball cleanly off the sand – but if he only thinned it, that wouldn't matter too much. Hitting fat in the circumstances would almost certainly leave the ball in the bunker, but a slightly thinned shot will get him out and down the fairway, provided he had a lofted enough club.

The Gentle Splash

In the bunker beside the green, Bob should be slightly mollified to see that at least he has a reasonable lie. He just needs to play an easy splash shot; nothing fancy. It's easy because you don't even have to hit the ball, which is forced out of the bunker by the build up of sand between it and the club face. It is *not* easy though because it takes a fair degree of skill to judge the right amount of sand needed to get the ball to behave properly – and this is what foxes the club golfer.

Now Bob could learn the right technique to play the standard splash shot quickly, and so could you. Applying it like a Tour pro might take a little time. But there is a *sure* way to splash out of a bunker, by setting up and swinging right.

First, Bob has to understand just what his clubhead should do when he swings it into the sand. He should not think of 'sliding it under the ball': although that is a fair description, it can and does cause confusion with some golfers. Rather, he should perceive the splash shot as one where the ball floats out of the bunker on a cushion of sand. A cushion some six inches long, three inches deep and as wide as the face of his sand iron, say three inches.

This is the amount of sand he has to splash out, with the ball as it were riding on top of it. To do this the face of his sand iron has to be open as it is swung under the ball. If it is closed, or worse shut, it will dig in too deep and smother the force of the shot.

So you need an open club face and stance, with the ball well forward and a firm grip. But turn your left hand. What helps you to get the club face open is to turn your left hand under, so when you look down you can see all your fingernails on your left hand. Put it underneath, push your hands forward and that way the club face is open. You move it back slowly and slide the club underneath. If you have your hand over, as if you're looking at the time on your watch on your left wrist, it is virtually impossible to get the club in the right place. You weaken the left hand, move the hands forward, open the blade and accelerate through the ball.

So the first thing that Bob has to do is to make certain that his club face is open. To do this, he stands by the ball and assesses where he wants it to land on the green and his target line. Then he opens the club face of his sand iron to that line and holds it in his normal grip, perhaps a couple of inches down from the top.

Bob must then set up with the ball well forward in his narrow stance, with his hands just forward of it and most of his weight on his left foot. The line of his feet and *shoulders* should point as far to the left and open to his target line as the club face is open (in this case some twenty degrees). He then has to swing back up and down along this line (of his feet) which being naturally out to in steepens its arc so that it impacts the sand some two inches behind the ball.

He has to make a *slow*, smooth three quarter swing with his arms, cocking his wrists fully and hit down firmly (not explosively) into the sand. If he then makes certain that he does not close the club face through the ball (that he doesn't roll his wrists, but keeps the right hand *under* the club in the follow through) it will pop out of the bunker on its cushion of sand, every time.

Using this technique, sticking with it for every splash shot from a good lie, will cure Bob's mental block about bunkers in no time at all – and it will do the same for you. An open club face, open stance, ball forward, hands ahead and a slow swing without rolling the wrists will get the ball out for sure. It is the technique every poor bunker player should adopt and the basis of that used by the top Tour pros.

Gary Player, for long acknowledged as the best bunker player in the world by most of his fellow pros, sets up in exactly the same way, although his action through the ball is not for the club golfer.

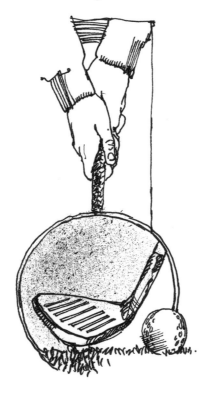

OPEN WIDE TO GET FULL LOFT.

Player opens his club face at address and fans it further on the backswing. His hard leg drive on the downswing produces a very long cut in the sand. In fact he can hit the sand a full six inches behind the ball for certain shots to ensure he gets it very close to the hole. But then, Player used to practice his bunker shots until he seized up and most of his rivals in tournaments would prefer to see him in the rough rather than in a bunker, as he was more than likely to hole out from the sand, as he still is.

How Far Behind, Open or Hard?

Many top Tour pros today have become very competent at getting the ball close to the flag from a bunker, if not holing it, and they are probably the ones that practice in the sand most. For it's interesting to note that there is a great divide between the top ten money winners and those in the 'middle of the pack' – and this is entirely due to the efficiency of their bunker play. Statistics from the US Tour in the 1990's show that there is little to separate the top ten from those ranked in the sixties when it comes to driving distance. The top players averaged 262.9 yards, compared to 262.5 for those in the pack: a difference of only one foot. The top ten were only less than two per cent better in hitting greens in regulation figures and just two one-hundredths of a stroke better in putting. The big difference (and the only real difference, which made all the difference where the money went) was in 'sand saves', getting it up and down in two from a bunker. With these the top ten were nearly nine per cent better, splashing (rather than driving) for dough, as it were.

Getting up and down for two is what the club golfer has to aim for whenever he gets into a greenside bunker. Getting out, yes of course, but you should try to leave your ball within an easy one putt range of the hole. However, judging just how hard you should play the splash shot to get the right distance is not all that easy if you won't practice very much.

Some golfers are advised (and so try) to vary the distance by the amount they set the club face open and stand open. Others try to vary the shot length by how far they contact the sand behind the ball; one inch, two inches, four, etc. There are also those who always swing down two inches behind the ball and hit harder or softer.

Certain pros also believe that the *amount* of sand taken (how deeply the club face enters) determines the length and so vary this by the position of their hands at address. This means that for a long bunker shot you need a thin 'strip' of sand, so the hands are set slightly behind the ball to give a shallow downswing arc. For a short shot, the hands should be well ahead of the ball, digging the club in deeply, taking a lot more sand, and just popping the ball out.

All this is rather confusing for the golfer and only adds to his uncertainty factor – so what do you do to simplify things? Well, let's look at these four options in a little detail to assess their use for you.

Varying the degree the club face and stance are open certainly affects the length of the shot. It has the advantage that you always take the same length of backswing and always hit some two inches behind the ball. Judging the right amount the club face should be open, however, calls for a lot of practice and when it's opened wide (say 45 degrees) the golfer runs the considerable risk of a socket.

Hitting at different distances behind the ball also has a plus or two, including the advantage of the same firm, three quarter backswing for every shot. When the clubhead enters the sand some two inches behind the ball (with a slightly open clubface) it digs down about an inch in normal conditions and its heavy base passes under the ball, throwing it up on a high trajectory. There is very little backspin created and, as the sand absorbs the force of the shot, not so much distance. You get more distance and backspin, though less height, the closer you enter the sand to the ball and if you were to hit just half an inch behind the abrasive action of the sand would produce plenty of bite. The trouble is that the club golfer, standing over his ball in a bunker, finds it very hard to bring his club down firmly half an inch, or even an inch, from it. He is far more likely to skull it into the lip.

As for varying the position of the hands, he is equally likely to misjudge just how far ahead, or behind, the ball they should be. This takes, again, a lot of practice, which is not on the social golfer's agenda.

So we come to varying the distance by the force, the feel, of our swing. Using the basic splash shot technique, with club face and stance slightly open, you can gauge the amount of power needed by relating it to your chipping action. Remember how you imagined you were bowling underarm with your right hand to chip the ball up to the flag? Well you can use the same method with the splash shot to get the feel – only you need to apply *twice* the force with the splash as you use for the chip. To give an example: if you had a ten yard splash shot, imagine the feel of a twenty hard chip. Put that into your swing and you could get very close.

GETTING PLENTY OF 'BITE'.

Up and Down in Two

So far, we've been playing Bob's splash shot from a greenside bunker, with a reasonable lie on regular, coarse sand. But what if the sand is soft (fine, or fluffy) or if it's wet and hard as concrete? Well soft sand causes the biggest problems, because it has little resistance to the clubhead and it's very easy to dig in too deeply and fluff the shot. All a club golfer can do is try and take as little of it as possible, swinging on as shallow an arc as he can and keeping his hands level with the ball at set up. When the sand is wet and very compacted, he needs to do the opposite: keep his hands well ahead and dig down deep. In this case, he would probably be unable to use his sand iron, as its sole would bounce on the surface and skull the ball, so he should try using a 9-iron to bite in under instead.

You also need to dig deep when the ball is plugged, or buried in normal sand. But in this case don't hood, or close the club face as many recommend. This does get the ball out, but it then tends to run a lot. Your set up needs to have an exaggerated open stance with your feet well dug into the sand and your club face should be open too. Try and swing back as upright as possible and then drive down hard into the sand, on as steep an arc as possible, just behind the ball. Don't think of the follow through: there isn't one. Just dig in as deep as possible and it's astonishing how easily the ball will explode out of the bunker, maybe even with a little backspin.

You will also have to forget any follow through if the ball is on a steep uphill lie at the front of a bunker. You have to hit closer to the ball than you do on the flat, as the sand is much deeper at the point of entry, which will slow up your clubhead. To limit any sway, sink your feet in deep and keep most of your weight on your left side. Hit down as hard as you can into the sand and the force of the shot should build up a sufficient cushion to float the ball onto the green.

WHEN YOU'RE PLUGGED, STAB DOWN SHARPLY.

If your ball is on a steep downhill lie at the back of a bunker, you are facing one of the most difficult shots in golf. But don't despair: the technique is not hard, it's just executing it right. As, on a downhill lie, the depth of sand decreases from the point where the clubhead enters it, you have to aim for a spot well behind, four or five inches behind, the ball. To avoid falling into the shot, you also have to keep your weight on your right side throughout the swing. Apart from that, just swing slowly with a slightly open stance and clubface and follow through without rolling your wrists. Don't worry about distance from the flag: in this case, as a club golfer, your sole concern is just to get the ball out onto the green.

The same is true really for all bunker shots for the casual golfer. Given you understand and apply the right technique to splash the ball out, the more you play, the closer to the flag you will end up. But while you are gaining the experience, you *must* get the ball out of the sand and save your miracles for the green! Getting down in 3 shots is not bad at all. Be realistic.

THE FINAL STROKE

I t is on the greens that most club golfers should feel more at ease with the game. After all isn't this the finest prepared bit of grass on the whole course? There you are lying clean and tidy on a beautifully tended green; all the stress of driving off the tee (particularly if there's another game behind, watching) or the anxiety about getting out of the bunker are behind you. You're 'on the lawn' at last, ah, that feeling of relief: after all, anyone can putt.

Or can they? Most golfers, when thinking about a round they've just played, remember the good shots and one or two of the bad, but invariably forget the several greens they have three putted. Yet putting is not just a major part of the game, it is another *half* of the game. It accounts, or should account, for half your shots, all played with just one club.

How many golfers really appreciate this and so try to 'groove' a repeating putting action? Well, some appear to, like Doug. Having prowled the line of his putt, concentrating furiously, he settles into a contorted posture, reminiscent of Rodin's thinker and squats there for twenty seconds or so, immobile. He is visualising a stroke where the head of his putter swings back in a neatly curved line (through position B to point C, as detailed in the book) before sweeping back through low and straight. His putter, seemingly with a will of its own, then staggers back in an elliptical arc and jerks forward, sending even two foot tiddlers right of the hole, 50 per cent of the time.

Matt, his 'regular' partner is invariably exasperated. He is of the 'miss them quick' method. On long putts, he takes a general line to the hole and then knocks the ball up towards it, hoping it will end up somewhere in the vicinity, so that he should be able to get down in two. He also feels that he could always be lucky, in that the hole should sometimes get in the way.

This is not such a silly way of approaching the other half of the game of golf, as there is a lot of evidence to suggest that *luck* plays a very important part in putting. Some years ago, the Golf Society of Great Britain conducted a series of tests using a special machine that could be aimed precisely to measure an optimum level of putting performance. It could strike a ball consistently on a chosen line at a regulated speed and in theory should have holed everything. However, while it did sink 98 per cent of 'putts' from a six foot range, it could only manage to hole 50 per cent from 20 feet. This means that even a perfectly struck putt may not drop under ideal test conditions and highlights the element of luck in putting.

It is not surprising that top Tour pros fare even worse than a machine. In the late 1980s, the putting performance of a group of US Tour pros was analysed and even their high averages for a number of distances under real conditions give the club golfer cause for thought. They sank 95 per cent of the three-footers, it's true, but they only made 55 per cent of the six foot putts and a mere 30 per cent from ten feet. Further stark details show a high average of only 16 per cent for 20 foot putts, dropping to 9 per cent for 30 footers.

Now the short range (three foot) and the long (30) don't seem too bad perhaps, but if Tour pros, who practice their putting constantly, can only sink 55 per cent of six foot putts, what hope for the amateur? Well, there is hope, given the luck element. Some golfers realising this can become positively inspired on the greens.

Bob is one such. Despite addressing his putts in a way that could scarcely be called a stance and with a very wristy stroke, he manages to sink putts from all angles to the consternation of opponents. The fact that he usually holes out when it doesn't matter a whit, is neither here nor there. His *confidence* on the greens is all important: he believes that he can sink every putt he attempts and this positive attitude is the salvation of his handicap, for without it he would be most unlikely to break 100.

Confidence is the key factor in good putting, but it is not true that if you haven't got it you will always be a poor performer on the greens. Your confidence can be increased by realising what the best putters do (and why) and by applying a few basic guidelines for developing a sound putting stroke. It is further boosted by appreciating the other factors that help to make a putt: judging its speed, hitting it sweetly, reading the line on the greens.

Finally, you should be positively cheered up by knowing the part that luck plays in putting, for there is no reason why you should not be as lucky as the best putters on any Tour today. So what if you miss the odd one, if it curls maddeningly out of the hole? Well, you won't miss the one coming back. If you develop that attitude, your putting will improve enormously.

Square to Square

When it comes to some basic guidelines for developing a sound, velvety putting stroke, the golfer should start with the one club responsible for his performance on the greens: the putter. The choice of the right 'magic wand' for you is mostly a matter of feel (as with your other clubs) but today it could also be influenced by the *style* with which you putt.

In days gone by, the wooden headed putter was *de rigueur*, as was the metal blade with the hickory shaft (for more feel) that followed it (epitomised in Bobby Jones' legendary weapon, 'Calamity Jane'). Since then, putters have appeared with marble, ebony or aluminium heads and a vast variety of shapes, like the croquet mallet, which was soon banned. Golfers of all abilities have bought quiverfuls of different makes, some pros owning up to owning several dozen over the years in their search for the perfect club.

Today there is a plethora of putters to choose from, with heads made of beryllium, brass, bronze, ceramic, cobalt, copper, steel or zinc – though it doesn't seem to matter which type you pick. Nor should the materials that compose the shaft – for the club golfer. The loft can be important, though. Most putters have a loft of between two and five degrees and the larger the angle the more the suitability for 'rough' greens.

Putter types, although sometimes hard to distinguish with all the weird and wonderful shapes on hand, fall into three groups. The blade (sometimes centre shafted) requires a very precise strike and is not ideal for the average golfer. The D shaped mallet, which has its weight behind the 'sweet spot' for extra feel, is also less forgiving with miss hits. The heel and toe variety though, with its weight distributed at the ends and with a heel mounted or near centre shaft, is forgiving and has a larger sweet spot to boot.

Which should you choose? Well, it depends whether you putt square to square, or open to closed. To explain further, you should first consider the totally different stroke actions of three of the greatest putters there have been: Billy Casper (virtually a wrists only 'popper'), Bobby Locke (a forearms stroker) and Bob Charles (a stiff wristed shoulder swinger).

In his heyday, Billy Casper set some incredible putting 'records'. When he won the 1959 US Open he took only 114 putts over the four rounds, 30 under the standard ration. When he won again in 1966, he needed only 117 putts (compared to Lee Trevino, another superb putter, who won in 1968 and '71, scoring 125 and 124 in each round respectively).

Casper, who believed in playing safe and unhurriedly from tee to green, became decidedly aggressive on the putting surface. Having read the line, by heart it seemed, he set up with a square stance and a reverse overlap grip, with the thumbs down the shaft and a medium width stance. He stood very close to the ball, with his eyes directly over it and he then placed his left hand on his left thigh, to steady his putting stroke.

Now generations of golfers have tied themselves in knots trying to follow the dictum of keeping the putter square to the swing path, while taking it back *low* to the ground. Not so Casper. He believed in eliminating the arms from the stroke (except on long putts) so he only hinged his wrists backwards and forwards, giving the ball a sharp rap into the hole. This wrist-only backswing certainly kept the face of the putter square to the line, in fact the putter head followed the line back precisely, but it wasn't low to the ground. Like a pendulum, the short arc rose well above the grass, while the follow through stopped only three or four inches past the ball's position at his address.

In complete contrast, Bobby Locke (the great South African) had a style all his own. Long and flowing, the club swung back well inside the target. He was considered quite unorthodox by his fellow professionals particularly when he was burning up the US Tour in the late 1940s and winning his four British Opens between 1949 and 1957. Locke was unorthodox, but the sound the putter made when it struck the ball was absolutely pure. He had a beautiful stroke that he managed to repeat time and time again, with his longer than standard, flat lying hickory shafted putter, which has a very slim well used leather grip. But he was considered unorthodox because everyone believed that Locke simply *hooked* all his putts into the hole.

There was some justification for this in that Locke, lightly holding his hickory shafted putter in a standard overlap grip, addressed the ball with a very closed stance. He did this to eliminate any chance of cutting across the target line from out to in, putting slice spin on the ball. What he wanted was to give the ball topspin, so he always positioned it off his left foot, striking it slightly on the upswing of his stroke.

His putting stroke went back well inside the line and Locke maintained that he always kept the face of his putter square to it, swinging his wrists, hands and arms as a unit. "There is no wristwork in my backswing", he wrote in 1972. "Wristwork in putting breeds inconsistency". Some of his fellow pros may have seen it differently: some believed that he opened his blade on the backswing, others felt that it was slightly closed. Many felt that he jabbed at the ball coming down, even taking divots. Whatever Locke did it, worked superbly.

Bob Charles, a New Zealander, who without doubt was one of the finest putters of all time had, possibly, the perfect putting stroke. A left hander, he putted stiff wristed, swinging his arms from his shoulders. It was the epitome of simplicity. He believed that it was impossible to stroke putts consistently well using the wrists and arms, particularly if you were playing all the time. As the big muscles of the shoulders are easier to control (and, in theory, immune to the yips) using them alone gave him a repetitive pendulum stroke.

So he set up well inclined over the ball, using a reverse overlap grip and simply rocked his shoulders back and forward, pulling the putter smoothly back and through on line. It was very noticeable that in his action the 'Y' formed by his arms and the club shaft remained constant throughout his swing, which equally constantly it seemed swept the ball away on line into the hole.

Now since those days of extremes (using only wrists, or arms, or shoulders) there have been many superb, if not legendary, putters who have blended the different actions. Jack Nicklaus, for example, who is a wrist and arm putter and who is possibly responsible for this being the way nearly all pros strike the ball today, as his peers copied his successful action. You never see a short, wrist only tapping action anymore, and the shoulder sweep is rare. Today in the 1990s,

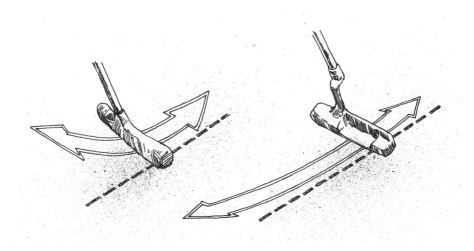

SQUARE TO SQUARE: OPEN TO CLOSED.

top putters use an arm action, with the wrists a little flexible on the backswing (to keep the stroke from feeling wooden) and the shoulders moving smoothly in unison.

There are two basic types of stroke though. One is when the putter head is swung straight back along the target line and then straight down along it, the club face being square to square. The other swings the club back in a flat arc, the club face opening on the way back and closing at the end of the follow through.

The square to square stroke is shorter, more of a hit than a sweep (reminiscent of Billy Casper) and you have to stand fairly upright over the ball. This means you have to be close to it, with your eyes directly over it, but you can position it anywhere between your left foot and the centre of your stance. Ray Floyd, who sinks them when they count, is such a straight line stroker. He looks directly down the line from the ball to the hole, sets up standing tall with slightly bent arms and arched wrists and uses a centre shafted putter. This is something you must consider in your choice of club: having the shaft more towards the middle sets your head more over the ball and promotes the straight back, square to square stroke.

Top putters like Ben Crenshaw, who use the open to closed stroke, set up a little further from the ball, with the eyes 'inside' it at address. Because he takes the club back in a fairly long, flat arc before sweeping it through, its face is only square to the target line for a very short distance, so the position of the ball in his stance is very important. He always places it opposite his left eye and he uses a heel shafted putter, which lets the club face rotate around the shaft, ideal for the open to closed stroke.

Few club golfers appreciate the differences between these two basic strokes and further complicate matters by employing parts of one with bits of the other. Brian, for example, sets up to stroke the ball open to closed and takes the club back well inside the target line. However, he lifts the clubhead well above the ground and in trying to square it (and get topspin) swings into a high follow through. The casual golfer would generally be better off avoiding the open to closed stroke. He should adopt and stay with the square to square method until he can consistently strike the ball on the putter's sweet spot.

The Sweet Spot

Given that most of the best putters today use predominantly an arm swing, with just a little flexibility in the wrists to keep the action fluid, do they have anything else in common, anything the club golfer can learn from? Well, for a start, they all have a consistent pre-putt routine, although this varies from player to player, and sometimes with the complexity of the putt.

Usually, a player will walk the length of the putt (to assess its length and the speed/strength of the stroke required). He will look back at the line to the ball from behind the hole, and on his way back to the ball, he will stop halfway to check the contours of the green.

Just before he sets up, he will take two or three practice strokes, gauging the feel for the right speed again.

Top tour pros have other similarities when they putt, as close observation on any tournament green would show. They set up with a stance narrower than their shoulders, weight evenly balanced, with the ball left of centre relative to their feet. The vast majority favour the reverse overlap grip, with both thumbs straight down the shaft and the left hand in a weak position to dampen wrists action. They keep their hands above the clubhead at address and many hook the right forefinger around the shaft for feel (like Seve Ballesteros, a fine touch putter, if ever there was one).

Many top putters also very consciously use their master eye, believing it should be directly over the club face, forming a right angle with the target line. All you need to do to find out which of your eyes is the master one is to simply point a finger, arm extended, at a distant object. You then close each eye in turn. One of them only will keep finger and object in line – and that's your master eye.

If you do not position it directly over the club face, at least use it when you're looking along the target line – and when you're doing that, don't just turn your head towards the hole. You must swivel your head along the line (so that your left eye ends up 'above' the right). This is particularly important for people who wear glasses. Unless the head is swivelled, they tend to see part of the line out of the corner of the lens, which can distort it.

Aside from such human penchants in good putting, there are four common mechanical factors in every stroke. These are: the speed of the club at impact, the direction of the swing line, whether the club face is open, square or closed to this line and finally the position on the club face where the ball was struck (i.e. was it hit on the sweet spot?)

Now only two of these need really concern the club golfer, who must not get so bemused by technicalities that he can't move the club. These are: the speed (strength) of the putt and making sure the ball is struck on the sweet spot.

With long putts, most golfers fail to get close through stroking too hard or too weakly, or by mishitting. The right strength is much more important than hitting the right line, although both must be right for the ball to drop. It is a fact that everyone misses the hole by a narrower margin right or left, than by the distance they are way past it, or more likely well short.

Many times though, when a putt is short it may well have been given 'enough', but (by mishitting) the sweet spot has not met the middle of the ball. The chances are that some putts will come off the toe of the putter, with a thin feel, the ball finishing right and short. Others may be struck nearer the heel of the club, feeling 'dead', and ending left and short. Only those struck firmly on the sweet spot feel and sound right and transmit the right strength to the ball.

Where is the sweet spot though? It is not always in the centre of the club face (and with some makes of cheaper putters does not always correspond with the maker's marks. But you have to know exactly where it is, so to find it. Hold the putter loosely by its grip, dangling down, and tap the face with the ball. The point where you feel no vibration in the shaft is the sweet spot.

Mark it well, use it when you line up and concentrate on stroking every putt with it meeting the middle of the ball. As for the other two factors, the swing line and club face direction, some tests have shown they are not so important in making a good putt. Besides

FINDING YOUR 'MASTER EYE'.

which, lining up and stroking square to square should take care of both for the social golfer.

Speeding over the Breaks

When it comes to feeling just how hard to stroke a putt, it's interesting to know that the ball is only in contact with the club face for one-fortieth of a second and that it skids for about a fifth of its distance before it starts to roll towards the hole. But this is for interest only: what is important for the golfer is that the ball is affected by the irregularities of the green (the scuffs, the dents and the spikemarks) only within some 18 inches of the hole.

Every time a golfer walks up to the hole and bends over to take his ball out of it, he leaves the imprint of his feel in a radius around it – not to mention, if he leans on his putter to do so, leaving a dent on the putting surface. Sir Henry Cotton once worked out that 200 golfers leave 2,419,200 spike marks on the greens of any golf course during a single day's play – and any one of those marks could deflect the ball enough for it to miss the hole from three feet. However, when there's an indentation on the green, it recovers. It certainly recovers on a firmish green. The indentation would have flattened out by the time the next group comes up to putt, unless the greens are very wet and waterlogged. There is often comment made of players leaning on their putters when they take the ball out of the hole. This, indeed, leaves a mark on the green but again it recovers quickly.

These marks do not affect the line to the hole, as they cannot be taken into account. But the fact that they exist must affect the strength with which you should strike a putt. Knowing that the ball will be deviated from the line as it nears the hole, when it is rolling at its slowest, every golfer should try to stroke it with enough strength to run it through the trouble. So be a bold putter. Aim to hit the ball so that it ends some 12 to 18 inches past the hole. If you do, it is more likely to hold the line and not be deviated by the war of the green.

Be sure that if you stroke the putt firmly like this, even if it is off line by some 10 or 15 degrees, it will end up only a foot or so behind and to the side, leaving a simple one coming back. However, nobody can *teach* you how hard you should strike the ball for any given distance. This is entirely a matter of instinct – and practice.

You cannot play golf by numbers and putting, above all, is a matter of touch. Yet some golfers seem to believe that the club should swing back a set distance for different lengths of putt (say, one inch for a one foot putt, six inches for a six footer, etc) the follow through being the same length as the backswing. But this method is too mechanical and you are very likely to jab at the ball with a backswing of only a couple of inches, guaranteeing you will miss the short ones.

The only way to gauge the strength for a putt is first to pace out its distance and then relate this to the feel for that same length you have in your mind from previous experience. This is why it's so important to have a few practice putts before each round. On the putting green, though, rather than just trying to sink a few at some of the numbered holes, pace out 20 feet and try to stroke the balls a foot or so beyond the hole. Keep the feel for the necessary strength in mind, and then try the same from 10 feet, before you make a few three footers to boost your confidence when you're on the first green.

Many short putts, of six feet and under, are missed through taking too much time before making the stroke. Miss 'em quick was an old adage. But you know if you make a study of the great players today, some of them take a long time lining up the putt, getting the

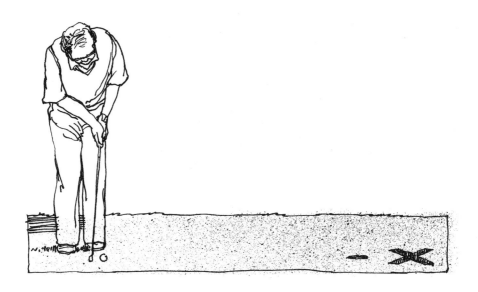

AIM TO END UP ON THE X.

feel of the stroke and once they're over the ball just give the hole one look. Colin Montgomerie falls into this category. On the other hand you have José-Maria Olazabal, who looks seven or eight times at the hole. Bobby Locke had a simple routine, one or two looks at the hole, Tom Watson the same. Jack Nicklaus used to stand over a putt for an enormous amount of time staring down, never attempting to take the club back until he felt totally in control of the situation. Afraid to miss a relative 'tiddler', a golfer can tense up and start worrying about the amount of break to allow for, despite having already spent some time deciding the line. As a result, he usually prods at the ball weakly, or, worse still, tries to steer the ball with his hands instead of stroking it firmly at the hole. Most amateurs in fact should hit their short putts a lot more firmly: it takes a very hard strike to get the ball to jump out of the hole, particularly if it drops in at the centre.

This is another important factor: some 90 per cent of club golfers aim their shortish putts outside the hole when it's unnecessary to do so. In fact, although the hole is some 4.25 inches wide, if half of the ball touches either side of it this is enough to tip its centre of gravity so that it drops in. This means that for a short putt the golfer is aiming at a target almost six inches wide (it is 5.93 inches to be precise, as the hole is 4.25 'wide' and you must add half the width or diameters, of the ball – i.e .84 inches-to either side.) With this large target, if the golfer aims for the centre and strokes the ball firmly he has a wide enough margin for error.

The Writing on the Green

This same arithmetic should be applied when judging how much to allow for a break with a medium length putt. Again, most club golfers over estimate the amount they need to allow for and so aim too far outside the hole. Look at it this way: if the target is some six inches wide, you have that amount to 'play with' if you read a break from the left and aim for the left side. You don't have to cope with a six inch break that often, so it's far better to keep your aim within the boundaries of the hole and just concentrate on gauging the right strength for the putt.

But just how do you 'read' the greens and judge the line to the hole? Well, there are three things that you have to take into account: the slope(s) of the green, the way the grass lies (in some countries this is very important) and its speed.

You start to judge the way a green slopes as you first walk up to it, as usually you can see clearly if it inclines uphill or downhill. If you're faced with a straight putt up or down a slope, well and good, although there is nothing simple about either. A large majority of golfers are *always* short on every uphill putt and equally run every downhill one way past the hole. Further, when you putt up a slope, the ball tends to curl off to the right, so to make certain you strike it firmly enough, with enough topspin to carry it to the hole, position the ball off your left foot and keep most of your weight on the right side when you set up. Conversely, downhill putts often roll to the left (as they are struck too weakly, closing the club face) so you should play the ball more towards the centre of your stance, keeping your weight over the left foot.

Judging how the green slopes across your direct line to the hole though is much more complicated. Some undulations are obvious, especially when you stand behind the hole and look towards the ball – and so are 'double breaks'. With these you must remember that the ball will be much more affected by the slope nearer the hole, where it is rolling slower, so allow more for that and less for the first.

When the break is not obvious and if you're not sure if there even is any break at all, you should first check the edges of the hole itself. If there is more wear on one side of the hole than the other, it will have been caused by previous putts spinning out as the balls will have curled off to that side, the 'amateur' side. Clearly, if you aim at the sharp edged (or 'professional') side, the ball is likely to drop.

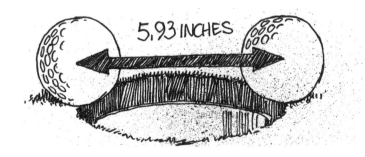

THE HOLE IS LARGER THAN YOU THINK.

Plumb bobbing is another method some top pros (like Ben Crenshaw) use to gauge the breaks (although it should be said that others like Seve Ballesteros, Jack Nicklaus and Greg Norman don't). But just what is plumb bobbing? Many casual golfers, not really understanding what they've seen on TV when pros dangle their putters and squint towards the hole, get very confused.

Well, the method is quite simple. You stand behind the ball, sighting with your master eye on a straight line through it to the hole, feet well apart, with your body perpendicular to the slope of the green. Holding your putter, with its toe towards the hole, lightly at the bottom of its grip, you extend your arm and let it dangle straight down in front of you. Then you lift the putter so that the bottom of its shaft covers the ball. Keeping it still, you next look up the shaft to the hole.

If the shaft covers both the ball and the hole, you've got a straight putt. If the hole however appears on the left of the shaft, the green slopes from right to left and your line should be where the shaft falls. Equally, you should putt along the line shown by the shaft if the hole appears on the right of it, which indicates a left to right break. That's all there is to plumb bobbing – except you must realise that it only indicates the way the green slopes beneath *your feet*, so it could only be applied for medium length putts and never works with double breaks. At best, it does give you a rough estimate of the slope, but you must still always check the break near the hole and find your line using *both* your eyes carefully.

In any case, the break that you read into a putt will not just be influenced by a slope, but also by the speed of a green. This is something you assess as you first walk on it. If the grass is soft or wet, the green will be slow and a putt may break only half as much as it would in 'normal' conditions. If the green is hard, cut very short, or even 'baked' as it sometimes is in high summer, it will be fast – and a fast green breaks twice as much as normal.

The direction the grass grows, the 'grain' of a green, can also strongly affect the line, depending on where in the world you play golf. In Britain, happily, the club golfer needs only to consider the slopes and the speed of a green, but in many other countries (in Southern Europe, the US, Africa and the Far East) greens can get very grainy and deviate a ball several inches away from the hole, even on an uphill putt.

If you're playing in these warmer climates, where different types of grasses grow horizontally creating the grain, you must take it into account when you are determining your line. Top pros playing there always check the way the grass is growing along their line to the hole. They look for shine off the grass, because if there is a sheen between ball and hole, the putt will be with the grain and so quicker. If the grass looks dull however, the grain is growing towards the ball and the putt will have to be struck more firmly. (This also occasionally happens on British greens, if the greenkeepers always cut the grass in the same direction, so be warned.)

When the grain crosses the line of the putt, the ball always rolls towards the tips of the blades of grass. Pros determine this direction by peering hard at the green, particularly around the hole, and sometimes by scraping the heads of their putters on the grass around the fringe (never on the putting surface itself). So how much break should you allow for to cope with the grain? Well, it depends on conditions, but with a straight 10 foot putt you could allow for a couple of inches break, while if the grain goes against a slope you allow for less break as the grain will retard it.

Choosing the correct line for a putt (judging strength, slope, speed and grain) goes a long way to sinking it. But the ball can still sometimes wobble off from the hole if it has not been properly replaced on the green before the putt is struck. To explain: every ball has a seam in it, which is quite visible on a wound ball and still exists with a two-piece one. Now although modern golf balls are truly rounded, there is a *slightly* flatter line around the seam, which gives a more accurate rolling surface along the green.

So every golfer, when replacing his ball on the green, should align it so that its seam rolls along the line to the hole. Just think of the care the pros take when they reposition their balls. How do you find the seam if you're not sure? Well, the ball manufacturers print their name and the number of the golf ball on an area at a 90 degree angle to the seam. So if you make sure the name is to the left or right of the line of your putt, your ball is sitting on its seam. Putt along the seam and it might just give you a truer roll into the hole.

One last thing. If your current style of putting looks awkward, if you sway, jab, stand on one leg, if you haven't the slightest idea how to read a green, yet you still manage to sink everything within four feet . . . please don't change anything. Just let us know how you do it.

PUTTING ALONG THE SEAM.

THE GAME PLAN

A great many golfers are captains of industry, senior executives or managers, at home in a business environment. They are used to setting a budget each year and creating a clear business plan. Each day they have to make tough decisions in the office, applying their expertise, creativity and common sense to tricky situations. Above all, at work, they try to avoid mistakes, for these can be very costly.

Yet these same people ignore all their background experience and ability in planning carefully and taking rational decisions the moment they step onto a golf course. They invariably over estimate their capabilities (getting into deep trouble when trying to avoid a hazard too far away for them to reach). Or they take risks (trying to pull off a once in a lifetime shot over a lake that even a Tour pro wouldn't take on). They never seem to have any plan of action (treating each hole as if they were seeing it for the first time, despite having played it on many occasions). They don't take external factors into account (ignoring weather conditions) and they usually don't choose the most sensible option (playing the percentage shot to the heart of the green, instead of over a bunker). Above all, they make mistakes, which are more to do with indecision than ability (changing a five iron for a six and coming up woefully short).

KNOW THE DISTANCE YOU GENERALLY GET.

Why do they do it? Is it a subconscious reaction to the pressures of the daily grind? Does it make them feel good to be *irresponsible*? One thing is sure: if they managed their business the way most of them play golf, they wouldn't last long in any company.

On the other hand, if they played golf the way they practise in management (planning ahead, weighing the risks, thinking positively) then the average social golfer's handicap would be 10 instead of 18.

For golf is a game of *course management*. Once its basics are understood, 90 per cent of the game is all to do with judgement and attitude. The trouble is that the vast majority of golfers only think about improving the 10 per cent (driving, iron shots, chipping, bunker play and putting) and ignore everything else, which they often are better equipped to handle. For learning to improve your swing, or your putting, requires a lot of effort and practice – but all golfers can improve the management of their game.

In fact, scoring far better with what you've got only needs the application of intelligence and common sense. You can easily prove this if you payed to play a round on your home course with your local pro, asking him to advise you on every shot as for the right club, direction and the shot ahead – rather than technique. If then you can master the non-technical aspects of the game and improve your course management, as a high handicapper you could simply cut some 10 shots off your score every time you play.

No More Guesswork

The first rule in course management is to know your capabilities, so you have to do an inventory of your assets. This means that you must *know* just how far you really hit each club, for without this you will never score consistently well. Now most golfers assume that they hit a 5-iron some 10 yards longer than they do a six, or a four 10 yards past a five, but this can be a fallacy, and much depends also on making a perfect strike each time. The only thing for it is to hit a series of balls with each club on the practice ground and be sure to note where each ball lands, because you must know how far you *carry* each shot.

You may be very surprised when you undertake this arduous, yet very rewarding, exercise. For even if conditions are good (dry, little wind, etc) as they should be, you will probably find you don't get the carry with each club that you thought you did (no wonder you buried the ball in so many bunkers in the past). On average, the club golfer will hit his driver at best some 230 yards, with a carry of about 180 yards on a dry, level field. He will hit his 3-wood some 200 yards, with a carry of 160, while his 5-wood (or 3-iron) will carry 160 yards, rolling a further 20 or so.

The other irons probably each hit some 10 yards less, with a decreasing amount of roll, 'around' the 5-iron, which should carry about 135 yards, rolling another 15. But pay special attention to the distance you really get with your 9-iron and pitching wedge. You won't hit the wedge *consistently* over 90 yards on target and you would be unlikely to strike your sand iron over 65 yards under good conditions. But you have to know your best distances (to make allowances in difficult situations) and once the guesswork has gone out of your game, just watch your scores come down as your confidence goes up.

You must though leave nothing to chance. You have to know all the relevant background details before you can create a business plan (size of market, types of consumers, distribution costs, etc). So you must equally *know* the details of the course you are going to play. You must know where the out-of-bounds are, the distances of bunkers from the tee or green, the local rules, the depths of the greens – everything relevant that might affect your play.

Tour pros (and/or their caddies) do this meticulously before every tournament, using measuring wheels or pacing out the distances on practice rounds. You don't have to go as far as that, but you really ought to have the vital background data of your own home course fully logged. It is not difficult to compile an easy to carry map of the course; you can note the key distances that most influence your shots as you play your next few rounds. And pay particular attention to the distances to hazards from the tee and the amount of room you have to work with around (and behind) each green. These are not often noted in the guides you can buy to popular courses, but the fact that these guides exist should also tell you something. They are not called 'strokesavers' for nothing.

Once armed with all this important background data, you are almost ready to plan to do business on the golf course. But before you start, there is a regular, routine preparation to attend to which will also boost your confidence that you've left nothing to chance. You must first check your equipment. Are your clubs clean, or are the grooves in the irons filled with caked mud and grass? It may make little difference to backspin, but psychologically you feel more of a golfer when you set a gleaming club face against a new ball. And how

CHART EVERY HOLE ON YOUR HOME COURSE.

about the grips: are they dry or tacky? A quick clean before you play will make each club feel in top condition – and you too.

Then there's your shoes. If they were soaked the last time, did you dry them out carefully (not on a radiator) and are any of the spikes missing or worn? Uncomfortable footwear can be very disrupting, so take a little care. The same applies to clothes. You must be sure your rig of the day will keep you comfortable. Temperatures can change a great deal, winds can blow up and rain can fall, both winter and summer, so you have to be prepared. No pro will set out on a tournament round without a spare sweater, an umbrella and a reliable set of waterproofs, as well as a hat of some kind. Nobody likes a wet head, or rain trickling down the neck.

All this preparation, which is little more than common sense, helps to reinforce a positive attitude, but a large majority of golfers scorn it. As a result, where they should be alert and focused on managing their game, they are often uncomfortable and unsure of what they are doing. So they only think about the 10 per cent of golf, the technical aspects of their swings, and multiply the mistakes, scoring heavily. Our fourball is no exception. Let's see how they tackled the short fifteenth.

This is a relatively innocuous par four, some 390 yards long, with a flat, wide fairway. A drainage ditch runs along in the right hand rough for part of the way and there is a dense copse of pine trees on the left, although both are well clear of the fairway. There is only one shallow fairway bunker a good 240 yards out from the tee on the left, while two greenside bunkers (left and right) guard the putting surface. Aside from a slope of thickish rough at the back of the green, that's all.

So how did our four cope? Were they fighting for birdies, while making sure of their pars? Well, Doug (with the honour) took his driver and smashed a horrendous hook deep into the copse, some 220 yards from the tee. His partner Bob, seeing the ball disappear and feeling he at least had to be long down the middle, sliced dreadfully over the rough into the drainage ditch. Matt and Brian, a little smugly, then played their drives down the fairway, 210 and 190 yards from the tee and safely on the right.

Doug found his ball among the trees, but tried to scoop it out through too narrow a gap, ricocheted off a branch and ended up in a worse place, with no backswing. He did manage though to poke his third shot out onto the very edge of the trees. Slightly blocked from the green, he then tried to hook his fourth onto the green, but aiming well right, the ball flew straight into the rough, pin high.

Bob hasn't seen any of this, being the other side of the fairway as well as being the shortest off the tee and so first to play. Pulling his ball out of the ditch and dropping it a couple of clublengths away though, he realises that he needs a peach of a shot to get to the green, some 210 yards away. So he strikes hard with his 3-wood and almost pulls it off. His ball ends in the right greenside bunker.

Brian, playing next, is very sensible. From the fairway, he plays his 3-wood and it is unfortunate that it just curls into the right rough some 30 yards from the green. Matt, however, feels he can easily reach as he has only 180 yards to go. So he pulls out his 3-iron, intending to hit it firmly. But he doesn't notice that his ball is sitting down a little on the fairway and so he only thins it about 100 yards. Fuming as he approaches it, he then isn't sure which club to take for the remaining 80 yards (is it 80? Or more like 90?). He picks his pitching wedge, hesitates, then 'to be sure' settles for his 9-iron. His ball, well struck, pitches past the pin and bounds off the green into the thick rough behind.

As they approach the flag, Brian is faced with a tricky shot as the hole lies over the right hand bunker. He could reach the putting surface on the left without too much difficulty, but it would be a long way from the hole and he hasn't been putting all that well (having told himself on the second that it was going to be 'one of those days' on the greens). So he tries to play a high, soft pitch just over the bunker from the rough – and ends up in the sand near Bob's ball.

Doug next pitches out of the rough, his fifth shot running well past the hole, and two putts for a most inglorious seven. He is joined shortly by Matt, whose pitch from the thick rough at the back just reaches the edge of it. His chip also runs past and his first putt rims the hole, but stays out giving him another triple-bogey. Bob, determined to do better, takes far too much sand with his fourth shot, barely moving the ball forwards. But he manages to splash his fifth some ten feet from the hole and, inspired putter that he is, sinks the next for a six. Brian, white knuckled, follows him out of the bunker in one, but then two putts, halving the hole. But the final score of two sevens and two sixes really is a little appalling, and if the four of them had each used a little thought, they could have shaved many shots off the total.

For example, when Doug stood on the tee he was very aware of the left hand fairway bunker, which would trap his ball if he hit his best, long draw. So he aimed well right and hooked. If he had taken his 3-wood and swung smoothly, there was no chance he would have found the sand. Also, when he was deep in the woods, he should have picked the widest gap (even if it meant hitting backwards) just to get out onto the fairway.

Matt made his errors playing off the fairway. He did not check the lie of his ball and tried to force a 3-iron when a 5-wood would have been the better club. He also did not know his distance to the flag and that made him indecisive, which is invariably bad.

Bob equally should have thought about the fairway bunker – and he should have known that even his best drive would never have reached it. So he should have aimed directly at it: with his natural slice, he would probably have ended up in the middle of the fairway. In the right rough though, with 210 yards to go, he should not have played a career best shot. He should have thought about laying up. An 8-iron from the rough would have left him with an easy pitching wedge to the green and he might have put it close enough to make a decent bogey.

Of all of them, Brian played the hole the most sensibly – and could/should have won it instead of halving. He only made one mistake: he did not play the percentage shot to the green when short of it in the rough. He should have looked closely at the area he had to land the ball in between bunker and flag. The green is long, but not too wide and if Brian had been honest he would have given himself a 30 per cent chance of making the shot. That is to say that with the amount of difficulty in hitting the ball softly from the rough and stopping it near the hole, he would have dumped it in the bunker three times out of ten, fluffed it just out of the rough twice, gone too far over the green twice out of ten as well – and only made the shot, at best, three times. On the other hand, if he had aimed well clear of the bunker for the fat of the green, he would have been on the putting surface about eight times out of ten, an 80 per cent chance. Had he then two putted, he would have made bogey, which would have won the hole.

That is not to say that Brian should *always* take a cautious approach and play the best percentage shot all the time. Had the match been all square at the eighteenth, for example, he most certainly should have had a go. But generally all club golfers would score a lot better if they weighed the options before attempting anything. This was not a very difficult par four. There are many others that are much more challenging and yet they can be parred, or birdied, by a golfer who does not have exceptional length or accuracy, but who does have a clear game plan before

ALWAYS PLAY THE PERCENTAGES.

he tees off and applies sensible tactics should he find himself in a little difficulty.

Tactics from Green to Tee

So how do you devise a game plan for any hole, rather than simply surveying it from the tee and deciding to hit it right, or left, to avoid a hazard? Well, you could do worse than to take a leaf out of the book of Peter Thomson, the cheerful, confident Australian, who won five British Opens between 1954 and 1965.

At his peak, Thomson had a simple, compact swing and always played well within himself. He was usually outdriven by most of his peers, yet this never bothered him unduly. He has said: "The most important facets of golf are careful planning, calm and clear thinking and the ordinary logic of common sense. Golf calls for logical observation. Beyond that the big thing is not power, but judgement."

He always had a game plan for the day and he always stuck to it unless he saw a rare opportunity to make a telling shot, which helped him to win many a tournament. He analysed every hole carefully, charting the hazards, working out angles and distances, allowing for different wind and weather conditions. He also planned how he would play each hole *backwards*, that is to say he decided where he would like to end up on the green, and then chose the best angle and distance off to achieve it, which depended on his own ability, with a certain margin of error. This pinpointed the area where he should hit his drive, rather than him making that decision when standing on the tee.

If you, as a club golfer, don't want to think backwards like Thomson, you still need to have a clear plan in mind as to how you will tackle any hole before you start your pre-shot routine on the tee. From the tee, you must consider three things: the club you need (for the distance you must carry the ball and where it will roll to), the weather conditions (especially the wind) and where the worst trouble lies. All three, in many cases, are interdependent.

Knowing how far you hit each club and whether you normally fade (or slice) it takes care of a part of the equation. But the wind conditions, which vary constantly, do need careful thought. If you

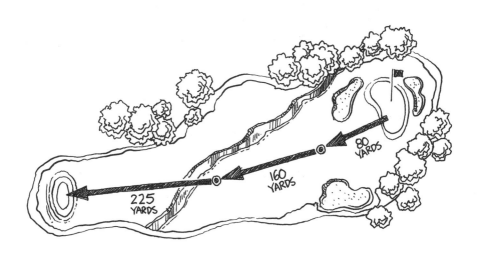

225 YARDS

160 YARDS

80 YARDS

PLANNING BACKWARDS CAN CUT SHOTS.

have to play into a headwind, try and keep the ball low (as if it balloons up it will slice or hook more severely) and expect very little roll. So take a stronger club than you normally would, grip a little down it, set the hands forward of the clubhead and hit the ball with a three-quarter punch.

Downwind, you must not try and slam the ball extra hard. You should tee it well up and make a full, smooth swing, letting the wind do the work. But you will gain extra distance (so really look hard at the hazards) plus accuracy, as the wind tends to straighten out slice or hook.

Crosswinds can be very contrary. A left to righter is not too bad for the hook: you can aim straight where you want to end up and let the wind straighten it out. But if you slice, you have to aim off well left and try and keep the ball low to avoid too much wind drift. With a right to left wind, the reverse is true. The habitual slicer can for once aim straight, as his slice will fight the wind and he may even hit the ball further. The hooker should aim right, again punching the ball with a three-quarter swing to keep it low under the wind. One last thing: if you are not entirely sure of wind effect, strength or direction, it's not much good tossing bits of grass in the air when you're standing on the tee. Look at the trees down the course instead: don't forget, your ball will rise at least to tree-top height.

Gauging how your shot could be affected by conditions leads to the next main consideration: trouble. On each tee you have to estimate how potent and how far off each hazard lies. An out-of-bounds, a two shot hazard (stroke and distance) must be avoided at all cost, as should a thick copse of trees, which could involve you not just in a lost ball, but with much scuffling among the roots. Lakes, streams, ditches and fairway bunkers, all one shot hazards, must also be avoided. But you must *know* just how far they lie off the tee. If you can't reach them with your Sunday best shot, it could make sense to play towards them and so avoid other less obvious trouble.

But don't dwell on any hazards: the more you think about them, the more likely you are to end up in them. So remember to hit away from trouble at all times.

Finally, on the tee, when you've made up your mind how the wind will affect your shot, where you will aim for to avoid the worst trouble and hence which club you'll hit to get the right carry and roll, don't change it. You must concentrate on the shot: go into your pre-shot routine focused on striking the ball well – and never try too hard to force or press.

If, despite careful planning and execution, you miss the fairway and find your ball in the deep rough you will only have one option.

You have to get out of it and onto the fairway by the safest possible route. You must not be greedy; just take your wedge and pitch out. And if you're in the light stuff and a long from the green, don't be greedy either. More shots are thrown away like that as you tend to swing extra hard to get the distance and fail to hit the ball squarely, crisp and clean.

In the woods you have to keep very calm. Do not try to smash the ball out, thinking you can bend branches (it's amazing how a pencil thin twig can deflect a ball backwards). Equally don't try to gain a lot of distance to (or even hit) the green if you have to thread the ball through several tree trunks. You may have read some pros advice to aim at the edge of the nearest tree, but ignore that. Just aim for the most appropriate gap and play firmly towards (and hopefully through) it.

What makes an appropriate gap? Well, it should be at least three feet wide if your ball is lying six feet away. At ten feet, it must be some six feet wide, and twenty feet into the woods needs at least a ten foot gap to be sure of getting out. Never forget, you are not Seve Ballesteros – although, like Seve, *around* the fairway, you have to be very aware of the rules of the game, which can bring relief from trouble. Remember that the 'embedded ball' rule works 'through the green', which means in the rough. Remember also the relief you get from the scrapings of 'burrowing animals' (although Seve failed to prove this case in the 1994 Volvo Masters on the critical last hole).

On the fairway, all the factors you take into account on the tee also apply, plus a few others. Supposing you've followed your game plan and hit a good drive onto the fairway, which gives you a good angle into the green. You've managed to cope with the wind and you know how far it is to the flag and the carry over any water or bunkers. But is the green holding, or are its approaches hard and dry? And is the fairway itself soft from too much rain?

GO FOR A GOOD GAP IN THE WOODS.

Water and mud can make a clean strike difficult and you may have to take a more lofted club, sacrificing distance, to make sure of catching the ball squarely. In really wintry conditions the ball doesn't travel as far through the heavier air, so you need to take a stronger club than you normally would. The green though would be holding well, unless it was frosty, so you must consider that too.

You also must think sometimes about laying up, something club golfers rarely do. With tough par four holes, the additional pressure of trying to aim for the green can lead to a lot of trouble: far better to be placed a full sand iron distance from the flag. You should also be prepared to lay up in front of water, as many top pros (and winners) do in the Augusta Masters. This is where your judgement of the best percentage shot comes into play – and, in the worst conditions, the safest shot is always the best one to play.

The lie of your ball on the fairway is also very important, as it can really influence direction – something which many club golfers, despite having played for years, fail to appreciate. If you are standing with your right foot above your left on a downhill lie, you need to select a more lofted club as a 6-iron will play more like a five, the slope cancelling out some of the loft. You then need to keep your weight on your left side, play the ball more off your right foot and aim left of the target. On an uphill lie, you have the reverse situation. You must take a less lofted club, lean a little into the slope and play the ball nearer your left foot so that the club strikes it at the bottom of the arc.

On a sidehill lie, when the ball is below your feet, it will tend to slice. So you must set up aiming left, standing close with a full length grip and your weight slightly back on your heels. If the ball is above your feet it will tend to hook. So stand a little further from the ball, grip down the shaft, weight on the balls of your feet and aim right of target. With all these shots though don't be too ambitious with length. You must avoid lunging at the ball at all costs and losing your balance. You should also take a few practice swings *in situ*, just to get the feel of how you should balance and swing.

But all this comes under the 'planning for emergencies' side of course management. Far better if you can avoid woods, water, and sand altogether and plan to hit your fairway shots from level lies. Tackling the par threes, fours and fives with this in mind from the start is the way to really cut shots off your score, rather than scrambling your way around.

Score on the Odd Pars

A good par three hole should always pose a challenge to the golfer, but it should also offer every golfer a chance to score at worst a par. It is very important to get your pars here and on the par fives. With four threes and four fives marked on your card, the par fours will do you less damage. On the tee, you have everything going for you. You are playing with the ball teed up, hitting a precisely known distance and you can usually see all the hazards clearly.

In most cases, your teeing tactics are important. Always use a tee peg as you want to be certain of hitting the ball before the ground and if the flag is on the left side of the green hit from the right side of the teeing area, as that gives you the best line in to it. The reverse is true if the flag's on the right – but often you should consider playing to the heart of the green if the pin is tucked away behind a nasty bunker.

If one of the par threes has an elevated green, plan to take a stronger club than you would normally use for that distance. The ball will not travel so far because the elevated green reduces the parabola of the shot. It's exactly the opposite when you're playing from an elevated tee to a green far below. In this case, use one club less because the extra drop extends the parabola.

Should you ever think of laying up on a par three? It might make sense if there is a large pond lurking in front of the flag and the carry is more than 150 yards. In this case, the social golfer has a better option of making par if he aims left or right of the water, giving himself a good chance of pitching close. And don't be influenced by the scornful attitude of your opponents: they could soon change it if they drive too far over the green or splash into the pond.

With the par fours, long or short, your first priority is to hit the fairway. Remember that if a stream or a cluster of fairway bunkers lie 240 yards off the tee and your best drive is only 230 yards, it is usually the best tactics to aim at them. When you're safely on the fairway though, the long holes (from 430–470 yards) are often beyond the range of most club golfers in two shots. So you must plan beforehand to lay up: to leave the ball on a level lie in a position where you can make a pitch that will leave you the simplest putt for par. *Don't* just take a 3-wood and slam away: you will almost certainly find yourself struggling to make bogey.

You can however consider the par fives as holes that give you one extra chance to recover – and still make par, if not a birdie.

On the tee, with a dog-leg hole as many are, the golfer is often tempted to go for the big, high shot over the trees, cutting off yards from the dog-leg and . . . *don't*. All par fives can be played sensibly, laying up for the third shot, which gives you a chance for a pitch and one putt. So plan a safe area in which to land your drive, resist the temptation of threading a long, long shot around overhanging trees to carry deep greenside bunkers, and instead pick out a level area from which you can pitch close to the flag. Remember that most par fives are designed with fewer hazards than par fours (their length providing the great difficulty for most golfers) and that the closer your ball comes to rest by that hazard, the easier your next shot will be. That's what your game plan for the course should highlight: it must put you in a position to play the easiest next shot, always.

Never Give Up

From the start you must plan the way you approach the game you are about to play. Unfortunately many people don't: typically, they rush up to the club in a hurry without any time to do more than take a few practice swings, let alone spend ten minutes hitting half-a-dozen balls to break down the adhesions.

One of the curses of golf is that it does take a long time. Squash and tennis are quickfire games and you can get a lot of exercise from them in thirty minutes or so. But not with golf. It's a slow, pedestrian affair and you must approach it sensibly. Before you play again, you must be sure your clubs are right and

PLAYING A RIGHT DOG-LEG, AIM LEFT.

that your swing is reasonably consistent. If you feel you need a lesson or two from your local pro, have half-a-dozen and 'pack them in' as quickly as you can to retain and build on your coach's wise words. Give yourself time to warm up before you play. Get as many things right as you can *before* you start – and this includes deciding on a clear game plan, which you must try and stick to with the best of your ability.

But the best laid plans can go very wrong if you have the wrong attitude to the glorious game. The trouble is that when a golfer hits a few good shots in a row, his confidence rises, he starts to hum cheerfully and he relaxes and swings well.

All it takes though is a couple of bad shots consecutively and the skies darken. His confidence level drops like a stone, he tenses up and starts hacking from trouble to even deeper trouble. What is worse, is that his negative attitude lasts much longer than his positive one – unless he guards against it and tries to be positive (and cheerful) no matter what.

If you hit a bad patch, hitting behind the ball and half topping it a hundred yards, then seeing your ball bounce sideways into a bunker on your next one, *stop* and think clearly. You should not let your confidence wither away. Both shots were within half an inch of being good ones – and your next shot could well be excellent.

Those of you who also tend to give up if you start the round badly, as so many do, there is at least one splendid example to help you view the remainder of your round positively. It was, in addition, set by a golfer in the Captain's Day Competition on his home course. Alan Telford, a ten handicapper, started *very* badly. He took a 7 on the first, which was a par three. Just think: four of his allotted shots had gone in the first five minutes. Yet Telford had the ability to look on each shot and each hole as a separate issue.

Quietly determined, he put the disaster on the first out of his mind. He then birdied the second and made very few mistakes in the rest of his round, finishing with a net 67, which was good enough to win the competition.

That is the example to keep in mind if your game plan goes awry, but you must make a clear game plan as soon as possible. It will help you to shave many shots off your score.

MATCHPLAY: THE LAZY
GOLFER'S GAME

It is extraordinary that the most popular form of golf, played by millions of golfers worldwide, matchplay, is only seen in a few professional tournaments, and that not every year. The World Matchplay (whatever its sponsor), the Walker and Ryder Cups (and the Curtis and Solheim Cups for women) provide rare opportunities for a golfer to view the game that matters most to him, or her.

The problem is that although matchplay is the finest form of the game, many pros dislike it. They hate being beaten in the first round, while in a stroke play event they could always finish strongly, with a rush of birdies, to end up high on the list. In stroke play, finishing second counts (a lot, with current prize money) but in matchplay, finishing second counts for nothing.

It is true that in some major stroke play tournaments there have been absorbing 'head to head' duels over the last nine holes. The British Open has produced some memorable encounters, like Jacklin v Trevino in 1972, and Nicklaus v Watson five years later.

Yet in these cases, as in many of the notable play-offs for other majors, like the US Opens, the protagonists were playing the course and not each other. So it is hard for the viewing golfer to appreciate any matchplay tactics employed, to learn from them the cut and thrust of play that lies at the heart of his weekly game.

But tactics there are, as there are (and always have been) some golfers who have shone at matchplay. Walter Hagan, Gary Player and Seve Ballesteros have blazed down the years to the 1990s. Hagan won five US PGAs in the 1920s (then head to head 36 hole matches) and beat the best of the world, including Bobby Jones, in other matchplay events. Player has to-date won the World Matchplay Championship more often than anyone else, and has some of the most memorable 'come backs' to his credit. Ballesteros has won almost as many Matchplays as Player, and has been the inspiration of European Ryder Cup victories. Each has embodied what it takes to be a champion at this form of golf: sheer determination, the ability to recover from difficult situations, to play a telling shot at the key phase of a match, to come from behind, and above all the absolute will to win.

Win Slowly

There are many lessons the club golfer can learn from these (and other) matchplay experts, which will improve their regular weekly game. They are all about strategy and tactics, which have the same basic approach whether playing singles (or a three ball) or when playing with a partner in a fourball, foursome or greensome.

In a matchplay singles, the first thing the social golfer must appreciate is that he is in for a *mental* battle. Never mind if he is playing a friendly game for a couple of balls or the drinks, nobody likes to lose. The objective is to win, fair and square, hopefully enjoying the play. If it is a friendly, the 'rules of engagement' should be amiable (no long debates on whether it is, or isn't, casual water etc) but you are trying to *win* the match. So the more prepared you are for it, the better.

This means that you arrive at the first tee well equipped, nicely warmed up and with a clear plan of the distances and hazards of each hole at your command. But you must not start by attacking course and man furiously in an immediate effort to get one up. Just get your drive in play. Don't hammer your approach at the flag, try and get it somewhere on the green – and be content to get down in two putts. You have to pace your effort through the match and the time to attack may come later. The worst thing is to take a bogey or double bogey at the start by trying too hard, find yourself one down and in trying to pull back struggle into further trouble.

Whatever some pundits might say though, you have to play the *man* and not just the course. But playing him by playing your own game, is not the same as trying to outplay him. Peter Thomson learned this lesson (and a great deal about matchplay) when he played Bobby Locke in a series of 47 matches in South Africa in 1956. Locke won 11 out of the first 14 matches before Thomson realised what was happening. "I was trying to beat him and he just sat back and let me beat myself" he said. "I was trying to out-drive him, out-approach him and out-putt him. It was all too much of a strain and I succeeded in nothing."

So Thomson decided to change his strategy. Instead of forcing, struggling to come from behind, he relaxed and simply tried to play safely. He gave away no holes impetuously, but made Locke earn every one . . . and suddenly he started to win. In fact, he won or tied the next matches until they were level, although Locke managed to get ahead 22 to 21 at the end.

The lesson for the club golfer is clear, particularly when it comes to trying to out-drive an opponent. If you find yourself up against a player who hits the ball a lot further than you do, don't try to out-muscle him, or even keep up with him. It puts too much pressure on you. In fact, the pressure could well be on him. As the longer hitter, he is supposed to out-distance you by far from off the tee, which should give him an edge, but to achieve this on every hole can lead to mistakes. You will also be hitting your approach shots first and if you can put these on the green, never mind near the flag, the pressure builds on him to get inside you.

You can however throw it all away and put an insidious pressure on yourself if you lose a hole to par, especially when your opponent is in trouble off the tee. This can stop any fight back you may be making dead in its tracks and often lose you the match there and then. It was the crucial point in the 1994 Toyota World Matchplay Championship final at Wentworth between Colin Montgomerie,

DON'T LET A LONG HITTER WORRY YOU.

Europe's leading money winner for the season, and Ernie Els of South Africa, who was the '94 US Open champion.

They ended the morning round all square and in the afternoon Els was two up when they came to the par four fifteenth, although Montgomerie was hanging on well and there was everything to play for. Then Els pulled his drive, ending up in a fairway bunker. He was in double trouble: he was well up the face of the bunker and when he got out should have been left with a long third shot to the green. Montgomerie just had to find the fairway, aiming then to play safely to the green for a par and a win. One down and three to play is not too bad in the cauldron of Wentworth and many matches have been won there from worse positions.

At this key moment though, Montgomerie, almost unbelievably, followed Els into the same fairway bunker, his ball ending even further up the face. He lost the hole in the end to a par – and the match was all over at the next hole. A amateur in that situation should have made *sure* of getting on the fairway, even if it meant taking a three or four iron off the tee. You must never lose an easy hole to par and, above all, throw away a hole your opponent is handing you on a plate. Elementary mistakes are often the most costly: they make all the difference between winning and losing.

You can also throw it all away if you take an unnecessary chance on a shot when you're ahead in a match. When you're up, going for the spectacular shot, the extra-long carry over a bunker near the flag, just is not on. Bobby Jones learned this lesson when

DON'T GO FOR THE SPECTACULAR SHOT.

playing for the US Amateur Championship in 1921. Two up on the eighth in his match against the British champion of the day, Willie Hunter, he tried to cut a dog-leg by carrying his drive over some trees. It was a shot he had played before with success, but this time his ball caught a top branch and fell into a ditch full of stones and weeds, from which he failed to extract it first time. He lost the hole to a par, the match on the seventeenth and knew ruefully that the eighth was the turning point. He had taken the chance, instead of making his opponent take it.

For indeed the one time you should take a chance, go for a spectacular recovery shot or flirt with water or sand, is when you are behind. When it is the last resort, when holes are running out, then you should try. But be aware, these shots rarely succeed.

Seven Mistakes a Round

Another powerful weapon in the armoury of a good matchplay golfer is a calm, unruffled temperament. He never lets himself get upset by his opponent, the rubs of the green, or his own bad shots. The classic exponent of this precept was Walter Hagan, who won 11 majors in his time. With it, he beat Bobby Jones on the only occasion they played head to head, over 72 holes in 1926, by 11 and 10.

Hagan played some terrible shots by all accounts, but followed them up with brilliant escapes and with a red hot putter (sinking 'one of them') broke his opponent's morale.

SO YOU'VE GOT SEVEN MISTAKES A ROUND . . .

Hagan blithely accepted that when he started a match he only had his game of that day, not the one of the week before, nor the one he might have the following month. So he had to make the best of what he had, which is why he avoided paralysis by any attempt at analysis. He also said he *expected* to make at least seven mistakes every round and so if he hit a bad shot he never worried about it, as it was just one of the seven.

He was also totally unconcerned about missing even short putts, feeling that it was impossible to roll the ball over uncertain ground with any regularity. So he just concentrated on making the next one, without thinking that perhaps his putting stroke might be wrong. Above all, he accepted good and bad luck as an integral part of the game, which is a great maxim for the lazy golfer.

It helps, to diminish mental tension, which can grab and demolish any golfer. Faced with an intimidating carry over water say, even if your opponent has landed in trouble, most of us feel tense and anxious. The club is gripped too tightly, the swing shortens and speeds up and a bad shot is often guaranteed. In this case, you should take the longest club necessary to get well over the hazard, concentrating only on where you would land the ball on the far side.

Were you to be in a similar position as Colin Montgomerie however, with your opponent in a fairway bunker a long way off the tee, then you should take a club which would never reach it under any circumstances and play the shot in a calm frame of mind. Facing the need to 'just get a par', you must play the safest shot you can and be prepared to take the 'rub of the green'. But it is very difficult at matchplay not to be jolted by a possibly lucky shot from your opponent, particularly if it comes at an important psychological moment in the match. This happened to Jack Nicklaus in his famous last round duel with Tom Watson in the 1977 British Open. All right, it wasn't matchplay, but it was the most magical head to head encounter in every sense of the word.

They were both level after three rounds (having each scored 65s in the third) and came to the fifteenth green on the last day in scenes of tremendous crowd excitement. Nicklaus was some fourteen feet from the hole, while Watson was off the green some seven or eight feet. But Watson holed out. It was a body blow for Nicklaus; a wicked punch coming at a key moment and probably it was then Nicklaus knew this was not going to be his Open, although he never gave up trying. And who will ever forget the sensational last hole, the 72nd, which was halved in three?

Nerves and Jitters

If you are not super-human, then you are bound to be affected by a 'lucky' shot by your opponent – but you should try very hard not to be unduly influenced by his behaviour otherwise. There is quite a lot of bluff around in matchplay and many players, amateurs as well as pros, are very adept at psyching out their opposition.

Walter Hagan, needless to say, enjoyed a good bluff. In the 1927 US PGA, playing Joe Turnesa, he came to the last hole all square. There, with Turnesa in good position in the middle of the fairway, Hagan pushed his approach shot into some tall grass, partially screened from the green by trees. Hagan then started to 'bluff'. The gap through the trees was quite wide, but Turnesa didn't know that. Hagan walked up and down several times studying his line to the green, selected and rejected different clubs, and finally waved his opponent back, saying he might have to play it safe. Then he hit his shot to within twelve feet of the flag. Turnesa, who had been kept waiting for quite a time watching the 'performance', must have been affected by such a 'miracle' shot, for he hit his easy one into a greenside bunker – and Hagan won his fifth PGA.

Now while such a performance is over the top and never really seen today, some golfers occasionally stoop to bluff, like hitting an easy 7-iron, and letting their opponent see the club, when an 8- would be the right one. Others go further into unacceptable gamesmanship.

Not any members of our fourball, of course. Being good friends they would never dream of adopting such tactics. Occasionally, it's true, Doug has been annoyed at Matt for 'shuffling about' on the tee when he (Doug) was about to drive. On other occasions Brian has suspected Bob of replacing his ball on the green nearer the hole than his marker indicated, while they all sometimes thought Brian had failed to count an extra bunker shot or two. But these are more

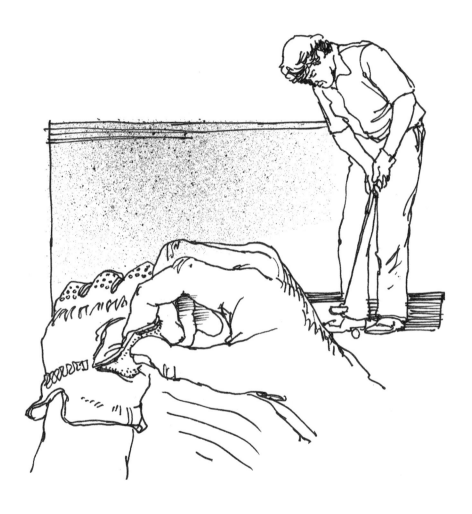

DON'T GET DISTRACTED BY 'GAMESMANSHIP'.

suspicions, unintended annoyances. None of our fourball would knowingly practice gamesmanship, although they all know a man at the club who does.

So just what is gamesmanship (as opposed to downright cheating) and how do you counter the main ploys? Well, Stephen Potter has amusingly outlined a few in 'Golfmanship' (invoking sympathy, proffering advice, and wearing the absolutely correct clothes) which are not so far from reality. But they are nowhere near some of the tricks certain players (including Tour pros) practice.

Some will deliberately make a distracting noise (clanking a club, ripping open a glove) to put an opponent off as he putts, which comes too near the knuckle. Others might stand near the right hand tee marker when their opponent is getting ready to drive, making him wonder if his grip, stance, or swing is being analysed, which can lead to unsettling self-awareness and doubt. Should someone try these ploys on you, the best thing is to step away with a smile and if it continues ask them to stop it, pleasantly.

Playing too fast, or too slow, are other deliberate distractions. An opponent who hurries along can make you instinctively rush your own judgement and shots, to your disadvantage. Equally, you can be driven to distraction by someone who lingers long over a choice of club or a pre-shot routine of many practice swings. The way to counter both is to keep playing your own game at your own tempo. Don't try to out-slow your adversary (as Curtis Strange suggested he would do when he thought he and Tom Kite would be drawn against

Bernhard Langer and Ken Brown in the 1987 Ryder Cup) and don't try to play faster than him either.

Sometimes though an opponent, wrapped up in a cocoon of concentration, will start to walk off the tee almost before you've completed your drive. Or else he will walk well ahead of you in the rough when you still have to play your approach to the green. Are these ploys? They can distract, if you let them, but you should try not to hit him with your second shot.

Above all, you should never be afraid to ask him nicely to stop doing whatever he's doing that distracts you. This is also the only response to one very popular ploy, where an opponent is always getting in your peripheral vision, taking a practice shot or three, as you are preparing to putt. Have none of that. Step away, ask him to move well clear and start all over again. Whatever you do never play a gamesman at his own game, play him at yours.

Playing as a Team

Sound matchplay tactics are equally important when you play in a fourball or foursomes game. You have to know your partner's strengths and play to them (as he does to yours) and planning a game strategy before you start certainly helps. For example, the steadier, if shorter, driver should plan to play first at the more difficult holes, which gives his partner more freedom and less tension to swing when it's his turn. When club golfers play however, they rarely think of the holes ahead.

One of the team will take the honour because he feels it's 'his turn'. If it's Bob, say, and he lands in deep trouble, the pressure on his partner Doug is upped unnecessarily and he is more likely to make a bad tee shot.

Much the same applies on the fairway. The golfer who has to play first should concentrate on hitting his ball as safely as he can into a good position as near to the green as possible. This gives his partner the opportunity to attack the flag – and on most holes at least one member of a team should be able to play aggressively. Far too often though, at a club level, both members of a team play as if they were individuals, each one seemingly trying to make a birdie on every hole and ending up with both scoring bogey or double bogey.

A two-ball foursome is a great winter game. Played by relatively good players it's possible to finish 36 holes in a day. It is also a great test of character although it is not so popular with the club golfer. It is the fastest way to play golf, can be great fun and makes you very aware that you are only one member of a team. For its one essential is to hit your shot into a position which makes the next one easy for your partner. But it is also very important that you are both in agreement as to how you play any hole, when to take a chance, when to lay up. This should be done before you tee off, as long debates on the course must be avoided at all cost.

With both of a team's balls on the green (in a fourball) the player furthest from the hole must get his within tap-in range, if he can. His partner can then 'go for it' with confidence. Sometimes however it might be more tactical to reverse the order. If the player who is sinking everything that day is lying furthest from the hole, he might ask his partner to putt first to see how the ball rolls and to give himself a chance of getting down in one. But both should be aware of how their opponents lie. As with singles, you must try never to throw an easy hole away, never to lose one to a par – and you must be aware of the state of the match at all times.

Playing as part of a team means that you have to be aware of how your team is doing overall, because in matchplay it can sometimes help you to win. Bernhard Langer, a relentless matchplayer, has always been very alert to the main chance for his team. He showed this ability to the best in the 1987 Ryder Cup, which was played at Muirfield Village.

Coming to the eighteenth, playing Larry Nelson, the match was all square and both of them were lying some three feet from the hole, having putted up. Langer then looked at the scoreboard and saw that the overall match score was Europe 13 – US 12 and he knew that to retain the Cup, Europe only needed another point. He also saw that in the last match out on the course, the one behind them, Seve Ballesteros, was dormie two up on Curtis Strange and certain to get half a point. So all he needed to do was to get a half himself, while Nelson had to win the hole, to sink his putt and hope that Langer missed his.

Smiling, Langer then asked Nelson if he would take a half for the match, as the two balls "looked good". Surprisingly,

Nelson agreed and it was all over. To make things even better for the European team, a few minutes later the inspirational Seve Ballesteros won his match on the seventeenth, which meant that Europe not just retained the Cup, but had won it again and won it for the first time on American soil. Keeping really alert in matchplay always pays off.

Lose One, Win One

Gritty determination never to give up, however impossible the situation might look, has also won many matches. You never know at golf. Sometimes an opponent might start to swing the club almost in a state of grace and score far better than he normally does, while suddenly on other holes his ball could bounce wildly off the fairway to end up close behind the only tree in sight, or plug in a grassy bank, or end up on the downslope of a deep bunker. You just never know: all you must do is keep on playing.

Gary Player is probably the most outstanding example of this positive attitude, this competitive drive, whether he was on top of the leader board or far behind in a match. One of the few golfers to win all four majors, he was also supreme at matchplay as he *liked* to beat people, to win. His determination lead him to staging the most famous comeback in the history of the World Matchplay Championship.

Head to head against the gifted American Tony Lema in a 1964 semi-final at Wentworth, Player was six down after the morning round and lost the first hole after lunch – 7 down and 17 to play, a daunting prospect. Surely the match was as good as over. Gary Player certainly didn't think that. He pulled back two holes by the turn and then won the short tenth with a par (a mistake by Lema who missed the green). In fact Lema lost several keyholes to par; the nerves were playing a big part. The crowds were on Player's side, the more they cheered the more uncertain Lema looked. Player gambled with his driver at the eleventh, hitting a huge drive which ended only some 30 yards from the green, setting up a simple pitch and a winning putt for a birdie. He gambled again by taking his driver at the difficult thirteenth and sixteenth holes to win them both in pars. Lema's confidence, by this time, was very ragged indeed and he couldn't control his tee shots. Finally, to square the match, Player risked all again on the eighteenth, hitting his approach close to the trees on the right, drawing it onto the green, close to the flag.

Now Lema was no pushover. He had won the 1964 British Open and was a considerable golfer, with a relaxed, easy manner and a seemingly effortless swing. But on the first play off hole his will to win was more than matched by an inspired, determined Player. Lema's approach hooked into a bunker and shortly after Player sealed a historic win.

If you, as a club golfer, want to win at matchplay you will have to show an equal determination to succeed. Do try to cultivate the same relaxed attitude as Walter Hagan . . . but whatever you do don't give up. You have to keep on playing.

PRACTICE FOR FUN

There isn't a golfer in the world who doesn't want to play better. To stand on a tee with confidence and hit a gigantic drive, to rifle a long iron to the distant green, to float a high pitch over a deep bunker which pulls up within a foot of the flag: these are the shots that mean you are playing golf, the way you feel sure you should be playing all the time.

But to have this degree of ability requires a lot more hard work than the lazy golfer is able, or willing, to do. He can cut his handicap considerably by concentrating on improving that part of his game that involves judgement and attitude, which is 90 per cent of it. Swinging fluidly and striking the ball better though seems far more important to the vast majority of golfers – and this 10 per cent of the game requires a lot of that dreaded word 'practice'.

Very, very few club golfers really understand what this implies. The practice ground at our fourball's club is almost always deserted. True there is a young lad, a keen beginner, who is sometimes seen at dusk spraying a collection of cut up balls in a wide arc.

Then there is a senior golfer, who potters along every day or so, hitting half a dozen balls lazily, before wandering down to collect them. The local pro also holds his occasional lessons on it . . . but that's about all the action it ever sees.

The members of our fourball have not practised anything for ages. Like 99 per cent of the other club members they have the (unspoken) attitude that anyone who practices is being a bit sneaky and is likely to be, at best, a pothunter. It is just not done, it is not in keeping with the true amateur (Corinthian?) spirit. Which is why Doug occasionally looks furtive when he tells the others he will not be joining them for a week or two as he has to 'work on his game a little'. What he means by this is that he will spend an hour or so at a nearby driving range, blasting two buckets of balls into the blue, in the hope that his acute hook will suddenly, miraculously cure itself. But that is not practice.

Bob, on the other hand, was more or less forced into trying to practice a few years ago when his wife and daughters bought him a practice net as a Christmas present. He suffered much the same galling experiences that Patrick Campbell detailed so amusingly in *Practice Loses the Lot*, having no idea where the shot he was playing was heading. The net now lies mildewing in a corner of his garden shed. And that was not practice either.

Know Yourself

Golf Clubs in Great Britain, in general, have very poor practice facilities: there is hardly anywhere to practice chipping, pitching or bunker shots. Most of the clubs which do have a practice bunker, should be ashamed of its condition. How on earth are golfers expected to improve when these facilities are so dreadful?

But what is practice? And how should you go about it if you really intend to improve the way you strike the ball? Well, the first thing to realise is that you should not just practice your strengths. This is what most golfers do on a driving range. If they can hit a 3-wood reasonably well, that's the club they use most to work their way through the bucket of balls. True it may lead to more confidence on the tee, but it does not improve the way a golfer strikes his long irons – and that weakness is one he should be practising.

The first essential then is to pinpoint what your weaknesses are. You have to analyse your game, honestly. Now in the US, where they keep statistics on just about everything, they have been busily collecting golfing data for many years. They have charted the performances of top Tour pros to high handicappers and can tell you that, under tournament conditions, the average pro hits ten fairways and nine greens in regulation, taking about 30 putts a round. An 18 handicapper however only manages on average to hit some five fairways and three greens per round and takes about 35 putts.

Knowing how you compare though doesn't really help you with your own game. What you must do is to note how you are playing over three or four weeks. It's quite easy. All you have to do is make a few notes on your card after you've played each hole. You should not be concerned with how many fairways or greens you hit in regulation, nor in the number of mishits you make or penalties you take. What you need to *know* is how well you strike the ball off the tee on average, how solidly you hit your long irons, how competently you play from the sand or chip from the fringe and how well you putt.

So when you're off the green at the end of each hole and the scores are being jotted down, take a note. For each shot you've just played mark down the club used and the way you hit it. If it was a good shot, ending up more or less where you intended, mark a G for good. If it was short, or a bit too bendy, yet ended up just off the fairway, give it an A for average. If it was a mishit, topped, shanked or whatever, put down a B for downright bad.

Marking how you played a par four, say, where you hit a reasonable 3-wood off the tee, a 5-iron that just dropped into a greenside bunker, a sand iron to some 20 feet from the flag and two putts could read: 3wG, 5A, sA, 2p. A par three, where your tee shot ended up on the back fringe, could read: 4A, 7G, 1p. Make sure you note down your performance like this on every hole (unless you have to pick up) for it will surely pay off.

The time for analysis comes when you're back at home and can look at the figures of how you really played with a little concentration. You will not be able to forget that you in fact three putted a few greens, nor that you took a couple each time to get out of several bunkers. But the chances are that your putting isn't *all* that bad and while you need to improve your play from the sand, it may not be the major weakness in your game.

It is much more likely that you will find (especially when you've analysed three or four cards) that, while you are a little wild off the

ANALYSE JUST HOW YOU PLAYED EACH HOLE.

tee, the major fault in your game is your iron play to the green. For this is the case with almost every golfer.

Whatever your weaknesses though, you will at least know them and armed with this information you will have a reason to practice. You can also give yourself a few clear targets to achieve, if you set about it thoughtfully.

Trials and Try-Outs

Now all Tour pros practice assiduously before and after each tournament round they play. They generally work their way through all the clubs, starting with the 9-iron and ending with the driver, before heading for the putting green. On each course there might be just one shot they need to practice for a particular hole or holes (like a high draw) and they will work on this more than any other.

Generally, if they mishit the ball at all, it will be with the long irons. With often difficult flag placements, there is a need to hit a long iron high into the air and get it to bite into the green. With every course there are also three or four critical shots that have to be hit just right to make all the difference, so these are the ones they practice most. For the rest, mostly 'ordinary' shots, the pros are simply fine-tuning their strike with each club and they believe that the more they get the feel of each, the better they will play the next round.

This is not the case for the club golfer. When you set out for the practice ground, you must only concentrate on improving your

USE YOUR IMAGINATION ON THE PRACTICE GROUND.

CHIPPING CAN BE FUN WITH A PERSONAL TARGET.

weaknesses. But the worst thing to do is to approach any such exercise in a negative frame of mind. You have to believe that it can be very productive to your game and that it can be *fun*, if you choose to make it so.

Your first action when you set your bag down on the ground is to make yourself a 'tee'. Dump your balls down in a heap (no badly cut ones though, please) and lay a club down on the grass, pointing towards a target in the distance, against which you will place your feet. You have to pick the target carefully – and you must know how far away it is, by pacing it out if necessary, or picking another at the right distance for the club you are going to work on.

Without these two basics, any practice is meaningless. Then you can start with a few warm-up shots, but you have to keep in mind just what you are trying to achieve. Are you aiming to hit your 3-iron, say, in a high fade directly at the target? Or hit 20 balls with your 7-iron that end up in a 20-foot circle around it? Whatever your objective for the day, you must stick to it – and don't try to overdo practice. Half-an-hour and 40 balls is a good workout: one hour and 100 balls should be your maximum.

The way the ball flies through the air is the important factor, not how you swing, unless you overbalance. Swinging to a high, elegant follow through counts for nothing, what matters is whether the ball was struck well, towards your target. You have to take your time with each shot and you should, with every one, go through your pre-shot routine (GASP). The more you get into the habit of this discipline, the easier it is to set up and align yourself right when you next play on the course.

Before each shot, you should also try and visualise, to 'see' in your mind's eye, how the ball will fly. Using your imagination like this is a great discipline, recommended by Jack Nicklaus, which helps you to strike the ball well. On the practice ground, to keep yourself motivated and have a little fun, you could also imagine that between you and your target you were faced with a long carry over a lake, or tall trees. When the time comes on the course to play a similar shot 'for real', it will be much less intimidating.

For you have to try and make your practice sessions fun. It is by far the best way to learn a lesson and a little experiment now and then with the club you are working on will keep you fresh throughout a practice workout. If your lack of confidence with your wedge, for example, is a serious chink in your golf armoury, you will have to practice with it. Now consistent length with the wedge is vital and it may be that you have no idea how far the ball will fly. Sometimes it climbs very high and falls well short, or else it bores quite low and finishes way past the flag.

So you have to experiment on the practice ground. The high shots could be because your hands are behind the ball at impact and if this is the case after you've hit a few easy shots, try moving the ball a little back in your stance. If this doesn't work, move it back a touch more until you find *the* ball position that gives you a consistent height and length of shot.

You can also try a similar experiment with your driver, although you probably shouldn't be practising with it unless you're a reasonably good player off the tee with your 3-wood. Let's say straight away that if you are and you still cannot hit your driver, do something about it. Go and talk to your local pro, take his advice, try out other drivers, but *do something about it* at once. Carrying a club in your bag you have little confidence in, especially the driver, is a waste of time. Anyway, assuming you only hit a few very scruffy ones with the club you have, don't just blast away with it at your distant target. Experiment. Try and shape a few shots deliberately right to left. Vary these with high fades. See what happens when you choke down two or three inches on the grip. But every time you are about to hit a shot, think just what it is you are trying to achieve with it.

Great Games to Score

One of the great things about golf is that you can get an enormous amount of enjoyment pottering about on your own. You can play one ball against another, try equally hard with both and see how you get on. Hit one ball with a driver from the tee, the other with a 3-wood and so on. Some golfers say, 'I can't practice long irons at my course, it's too short'. That's rubbish. All you have to do if you want to practice your three or four irons or even three and five woods, is to take a seven or eight iron off the tee. Imagine, you've got a hole 340 yards long, if you hit 150–160 yards from the tee, you've then got a long shot to the green. A small target, concentrating your mind on the job in hand. On the other hand, if you have a long par four of 460 yards, why not play two 5-irons and then see what you're left with for a third shot. You can ring the changes continuously and there's no excuse to say, because your course is short in yards, you can't play full shots to the green. Use your imagination.

You can also introduce an element of competition into meaningful practice to keep yourself sharp. Once you've achieved, or near enough, your target for the day, you should try and 'wind down' with a few variations, using different clubs. To keep this part of the workout interesting mentally, you can try to compete against yourself in a way that will still help you to learn a few lessons.

One absorbing practice game is to play two balls with each of your clubs, always aiming towards your target. The first ball you should strike with the best of your ability, allowing yourself a Mulligan if you mishit badly. Likewise with the second ball, which you should always try to strike with three quarters of your strength. Wager a mental pint on which strength of shot will consistently give you the most effective results . . . and you may well lose your bet.

Another wind down game is to mentally play two or three holes that you know well on your home course (with or without the three quarter strength swing). Pick a long par four, say, and imagine you're teeing off, so take your drive and aim it at your target. Follow this with your 3-iron and then play your wedge for the last 80 yards (obviously you don't putt out).

You can then pick a par three and hit a smooth 4-iron 'to the green', then follow this with a par five, which needs a driver, 3-wood and an 8-iron. In fact, you could 'play your way round' your course, in your mind, but the complete 18 holes is a little too much for a wind down practice session.

With bunker practice, one of the most important things is to get a club that suits you. Most people play their golf at their home club, unless they're in a team and play away matches or take their clubs on holiday. Bearing that in mind, see what texture of sand you have in the bunkers. If it's very soft and deep you need a club with a big flange; if it's hard and clay like, you will get better results with a thinner soled club. All these things are fairly simplistic and if you ask your professional the right questions, you should get the right answers. If in doubt, ask for a second or even third opinion. Remember when you're trying to get out of a bunker, your stance should be open, the ball opposite the left foot, the back of the club should almost be resting on the sand with the hands forward. The wrists then break quickly and go out, away from the body. You slice under the ball. You have a full swing and a full follow through. You hit under the ball very hard. If your club is swinging at the correct angle, the harder you hit it will only result in the ball going higher. It is basically fear that stops most people from even getting out of a bunker.

Practising in a bunker (if your club has a practice one) is absolutely invaluable. Just playing a series of basic splash shots at the pin is reward enough when it comes to building confidence. But if you want to add a little mental competition, you should try to line up six to ten balls in the bunker, each with a good lie. Splash the first one out towards the flag, but just onto the green.

Then splash the second ball just beyond it, if you can – and keep on trying to make the others each end up a little nearer to the flag each time. It is not as easy as it seems, for you really have to concentrate, but it is a very good game to give you a feel for the distance you splash out. Above all, it gives you a lot of confidence when you next play a round and find yourself in greenside sand.

You can apply the same rules in a similar game with your 7-iron, chipping from the fringe. Rather than just having a few stabs in the general direction of the hole, try and place each ball nearer and nearer it. Or you can try to see how close you get to the hole with three balls, using your 7-iron – and then try another series of three, using your eight. The more variations like this you can inject into your practice sessions, the more interesting they will be and the more ready you will be to play good golf after them.

Practising on the course

When solitary practice palls, as it will (even though you made yourself do it in the first place) the best remedy is to try a little practice on the course itself. Now let's say right from the start, you must never inconvenience any of your peers. So any such games must be played on days and at the time of day when the course is virtually empty. You have also heard that you should save any tinkering for the practice – and that's true as well. But sometimes you can brighten up your 10 per cent game considerably by trying out a few things on the course and, in this case, preferably with a partner.

Now finding someone to go out with you on a 'practice' round, who will join in the games you intend to try out, is a little like going on a diet. Whenever Brian's wife, for instance, goes on a new diet (which happens about every six weeks or so) she inveigles him to join her on it, despite the fact that he's the last person who needs to lose weight. However, as he never has the option (for she won't cook him anything different from the onion purée or whatever it is she's eating) he stoically has to comply.

You, however, should not have such a problem if you a) seek out a partner who is someone you play with regularly and b) arouse his interest in the type of game you want to play. For you will both benefit from the experience.

For starters, you could play the 'one club challenge'. This was a series on the BBC many years ago, in which two pros and two celebs were each only allowed to choose one club to play nine holes, using it for all their shots. They usually picked a 5-iron, although one or two used a four. If they landed up in the rough or in a bunker, it was all the same. They had to open the club face and play the ball out.

Now this is an absorbing exercise to play against an opponent. For one thing, it teaches you both a great deal about how to use a golf club and about how to play a variety of strokes. For another, it is invariably surprising how well you score with just one club. You may find yourself playing at least to your handicap – and the competition between you will be fun.

Brian, Bob, Doug and Matt played over the last Christmas break in a one club competition. The inspiration of their new club secretary, it was called the *One Club, Fourball, Betterball Challenge.* Starting at 10 am, after a warming drink or two in the clubhouse, two teams of golfers drove off at the same time on every hole on the course to play whatever nine holes lay ahead of them.

Having twisted the secretary's arm, our fourball all played together, Bob (for once) teaming up with Matt and Brian partnering Doug. Matt chose a 4-iron as his one club, with the idea that they needed a degree of length to cope with the demanding par fives. Bob played with a 7-iron, feeling that its left could possibly straighten out his slice (which it did) and that it would make it easier for him to get out of bunkers (which it didn't.)

Brian and Doug both wielded 5-irons and each carried a secret 'weapon': a large hip flask filled with Whisky Mac (to keep out the cold.) These they intended to quaff from on every tee (sharing, of course, with their friendly rivals.) They were confident that even if they did not win the competition, they would win the side-bets, as they had harder heads than either Bob or Matt. They were mistaken.

From the start, on the first hole they played, Bob and Matt were both on the green in three and Bob, striking his ball with the bottom edge of his club, sank the putt for a par. On the next Matt responded with a birdie, having held his club at the bottom of its grip to play a delicate approach which left him with a tap-in. After six holes, their better ball score was level par and they were striding along the fairway, whistling (maybe because of the Whisky Macs) and believing they might just win the Challenge. They had discovered that their choice of club had kept both of them short of real trouble, which is the greatest wrecker of scores, and that while the mechanics

ONE CLUB FUN. DO WE NEED MUCH MORE?

of putting with the edge of the club appeared to be much harder, it seemed to work.

Brian and Doug were faring almost as well, if a little differently. Doug, secure in the knowledge that his long-suffering wife was picking them all up from the club after the competition (so that all could drink festively and not drive) indulged a little too much from his hip flask. After three holes he suddenly developed a serious slice, which so surprised him that he started to chuckle every time be struck the ball, causing Bob and then Matt to accuse him of gamesmanship. Brian however played splendidly. Despite the piercing wind, he strung together a sequence of pars which, coupled with a flukey birdie of Doug's put their better ball score at one over par after six holes played.

All seemed set fair for both teams . . . but then on the seventh Bob and Matt started to find the sand, regularly. With ease, they both notched up a treble bogey, following it with another on their eight. By the time they had both got out of the same greenside bunker on their final hole, their combined better ball score was not much to boast about, although it still seemed quite respectable to them.

Their rivals at first exulted, then slumped. The penultimate hole proved critical. Doug alternated his new-found slice with his usual viscious hook and zig-zagged from rough on the right to rough on the left, finally carding a four over par. Brian matched him, losing one ball (very unusual for him) on his drive – and then losing another over the green.

It made no difference that they both parred the last. "One hole. Just one hole . . . wrecked my best, or possibly best, score . . . ever," said Brian as they ambled merrily towards the clubhouse. Doug chuckled in agreement, wondering if his new slice would be a permanent feature of his game – and one he could count on.

All our heros in the end, regaling themselves in the clubhouse amid general merriment, found themselves very satisfied. Bob and Matt had finished sixth in the order of merit, while Brian and Doug

BRIAN WITH PETER ALLIS, DOUG, BOB AND MATT

were tenth ("But we only *just* didn't win", said Brian.) They all agreed that it had been a really interesting experience, one that they had enjoyed enormously and they all felt that the Whisky Macs had made their swings noticeably more fluid.

Another game to try out, with your full set of clubs, is the one of 'endless Mulligans'. With this game, every time you hit a bad shot you take a Mulligan, play the shot again without penalty. This builds confidence in your swing, as it takes away all the tension of mis-hitting the ball, which wrecks the rounds and fun of so many golfers. You will certainly score much better too and the competition between you and your opponent should be very interesting.

The 'no hazards' practice game will also improve your score, probably by at least 10 shots. In this variation, whenever you get into trouble, be it woods, water, rough or sand, you are allowed to drop the ball out onto the fairway without any penalty. Now while this may not help you to practice your recovery or splash shots, it will help you to swing away with confidence. You will also enjoy the round a lot more when you see how well you've scored, as the chances are your card(s) will be spattered with pars.

Two ball practice games also let you realise what you are capable of playing like, given more expertise in recovery shots. In this variation, you both play two balls for every shot (not the putts) and pick the position of the best one to play the next two shots from. Once again, it helps to build up your confidence on the course, which is what practice is all about. However, if you really want a challenge, you could both try to play your 'worst' ball, which makes you concentrate hard as you have to hit two very good shots from every position.

Play off the tee with a three, five, or even seven iron. This way, you can practice many different second shots to the green on a hole of 320 to 450 yards length. A short course need not hamper your chance to practice long iron or wood approach shots. With such 'games', you could have a lot of pleasure when you need to practice. May you always enjoy the game itself every time you play . . .

INDEX